Ultimate

party drinks

Maria Costantino

Ultimate

party drinks

Maria Costantino

D&S
BOOKS

© 2007 D&S Books Ltd

D&S Books Ltd
Kerswell,
Parkham Ash, Bideford
Devon, England
EX39 5PR

e-mail us at:-
enquiries@dsbooks.fsnet.co.uk

This edition printed 2007

ISBN 13 – 978-1-903327-68-5

Book Code: DS0191. Ultimate Party Drinks

Material from this book previously appeared in The Cocktail Handbook and The Shots and Shooters Handbook.

Creative Director: Sarah King
Project Editor: Paul Stewart-Reed
Designer: Debbie Fisher & Co

Printed in Thailand

1 3 5 7 9 10 8 6 4 2

contents

introduction to cocktails

For thousands of years, drinking has been part of merrymaking. The practice of mixing drinks – whether with juices, water or with other spirits and liqueurs – is probably just as ancient. Although we may think of cocktails as being 'modern', by definition, a cocktail is a blend of two or more different drinks, so it may well have been the ancient Egyptians, Greeks or Romans who first made them, although their motives may well have had more to do with creating health-imparting elixirs!

The first documented mixed drink dates from the Middle Ages: in the 14th century, a 'bragget' was a mix of mead (a honey-based liqueur still made in parts of England) and ale. Many of the liqueurs used in cocktails today – such as the famous Benedictine and Chartreuse – have their origins in the late Middle Ages, when monks were herbalists and apothecaries, administering to the sick with their medicinal tinctures and elixirs. While the Europeans can lay claim to developing the complex distillation, maceration and infusion techniques for making the spirits used in cocktails today, it was in the United States that the word 'cocktail' first appeared, in a dictionary of 1803.

While defined as a 'mixed drink of a spirit, bitters and sugar', debate rages over the exact origins of the word 'cocktail': does it derive from the red cock's feather worn in the hats of the big winners on the gambling boats of the Mississippi? Did it originate with Betsy Flanagan, who served chicken dinners to American and French soldiers fighting in the Revolutionary War and after-dinner drinks decorated with the bird's tail feathers to shouts of '*Vive le cock tail!*'? Or perhaps it was the French Creole apothecary Antoine Peychaud who gave us the word, having, during the 1790s in New Orleans, measured out the spirits for his medicines in a *cocquetier* (an egg cup).

Whatever their origins, the craze for these fabulous concoctions soon spread abroad. Harry MacElhone opened Harry's New York Bar in Paris in 1923. Harry's Bar would be the birthplace of the 'bloody Mary', just one of the classic creations of this cocktail-barman *extraordinaire*. Even when Prohibition hit the United States, there was to be no let-up in the craze for cocktails. Americans who could afford to travel visited Europe, skipped across the border to Mexico or found solace in the Caribbean. For those who didn't travel, a pretty regular and plentiful supply of booze was available courtesy of bootleggers and illegal, bathtub stills!

The varying degrees of quality of illegal liquor available in the United States during Prohibition did not hinder the cocktail: in fact, to disguise the 'rough' nature of the spirits, cocktail-barmen became more ingenious and more inspired. The 1920s and the 1930s were truly the golden age of the cocktail, and interest in cocktails has not diminished since then. Generations of drinkers, inspired by foreign travel and new tastes, have encouraged the creation of new drinks – often with some quite outrageous names and combinations. Only when ordering a cocktail can you get away with asking a complete stranger for a 'slow, comfortable screw up against a wall', some 'sex on the beach' or even requesting the 'manager's daughter'!

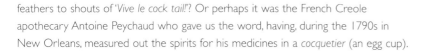

cocktail basics

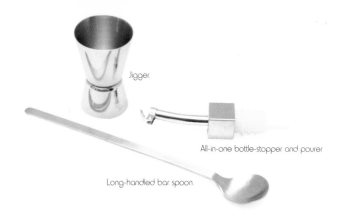

Jigger

All-in-one bottle-stopper and pourer

Long-handled bar spoon

You don't have to be a professional bartender to make a cocktail, but like for any 'art', it helps to have the right tools to do the job properly.

measures

The recipes in this book use one measure or half a measure of a spirit or liqueur. The word 'measure' is used because of the slight variation between metric, British imperial and US measurements (because each side of the Atlantic has a variation on the fluid ounce). Since most of the classic cocktails were invented in America, the 'jigger' used in bars in the United States is often a common measurement. It really doesn't matter what 'jigger' you use – you could use a shot glass, or even an egg cup – as your 'measure'. Just make sure that you use the same measure throughout, and the ratios of one spirit to another in any drink will be correct. One good idea is to measure the total quantities of a drink in water before starting, to make sure that all of the ingredients fit in your chosen glass! Don't forget, though, that shaking, stirring and blending with ice will dilute and increase the volume of the finished drink.

ice

You can't make cocktails without ice, and because ice is a vital ingredient, it is important that you don't skimp on it. You will need ice cubes, broken ice or crushed ice, depending on the cocktail that you select. The object is almost to freeze the drink, while breaking down and combining the ingredients.

Broken ice is easy to make: put some whole ice cubes into a clean, polythene bag and hit them with a rolling pin! The aim is to break each ice cube into three pieces. If you want crushed ice, you can keep on hitting, or you can put broken ice into a blender. Most of the blenders available can do this, and some make a feature of their ice-crushing abilities. Ice will melt quickly, so make broken and crushed iced immediately before use, and help the cocktail-making process along by chilling the drinking glasses.

chilling glasses

The simple rule for making cocktails is 'chill before you fill'! There are three ways to make glasses cold, as follows.

1 Put them in the fridge or freezer for a couple of hours before using them. This is not advisable for fine crystal glasses, however, which may shatter.

2 Fill them with crushed ice before using them. Discard the ice and shake out any water before pouring in the drink.

3 Fill them with cracked ice and stir it around a little before discarding it and pouring in the drink.

mixing terminology

When a recipe tells you to add the ingredients to a shaker, glass or blender, get into the habit of putting in the cheapest ingredients first! Put lemon or lime juice, sugar syrup and fruit juices in first, then the more valuable spirits and liqueurs. If you make a mistake, chances are that it will be the less expensive ingredients that are then wasted.

Never shake a drink with carbonated mixers – ginger ale, tonic or soda water – or champagne! This type of ingredient is left right until the end, and is used to 'finish' a drink.

Where a method says 'shake and strain', half-fill the shaker with clean ice cubes, add the ingredients and shake briskly, until the outside of your shaker is very cold. Immediately pour the liquid through the strainer, leaving the ice behind. The volume of liquid will have increased because some of the ice will have melted and blended with the other ingredients. Remember this, to avoid producing more drink than your glass will hold.

Don't shake and strain with crushed ice: the crushed ice will just get stuck in the strainer holes and will clog them up. Drinks shaken with crushed ice are poured 'unstrained' into a glass. Where a method says 'shake and pour unstrained', add a glassful of ice to the shaker, pour in

the ingredients and shake. Pour the drink into the same size of glass that you used to measure the ice.

Where a recipe instructs you to 'stir and strain', half-fill the mixing glass, or the bottom half of your shaker, with ice cubes, add the ingredients and stir with a long-handled bar spoon for 10 to 15 seconds. Use a Hawthorn strainer, the strainer part of your shaker or a fine-mesh sieve to pour the drink through it and into the glass.

Where the method advises you to 'stir and pour unstrained', prepare your cocktail as above, but only use a glassful of ice and don't strain the liquid. Add of all the contents to a glass the same size as the one that you used to measure the ice.

To 'build', you create the drink directly in the glass in which it will be served. Some drinks are built 'over ice' – the ice cubes are added to the glass first and the liquors added – others are made as a 'pousse-café'. A pousse-café makes use of the difference in the 'weights' of liqueurs and spirits so that one sits on top of the other in separate, often coloured, layers. This can be a little fiddly to achieve at first, but the results can be spectacular. The trick is to pour the liquor very slowly over the back (the rounded side) of a small spoon, or down the twisted stem of a long-handled bar spoon, so that it sits on top of the first layer very gently.

Pour drinks as soon as you have made them or they will 'wilt', become too diluted with melted ice, or, in some instances, separate into their component parts

When a recipe calls for a 'twist of lemon, lime or orange peel', rub a narrow strip of peel around the rim of the glass to deposit citrus oil on it. Then twist the peel so that the oil – usually one very small drop – falls into the drink. In some recipes, you should also drop the peel into the glass, while in others, you should discard it.

A 'sugar-', 'salt-' or 'coconut-' rimmed glass is prepared by moistening the rim with a little lemon or lime juice and then dipping the rim into the condiment.

Keep your ingredients cool: chill juices and mixers, champagnes and vermouths. Akavits and vodkas are best if they are very cold.

Wash mixing equipment between making different cocktails to avoid mixing flavours. Rinse spoons and stirrers, too!

Have all of your equipment – can-opener, bottle-opener, shaker, jigger, mixing glass, bar spoon, straws and stirrers – ready to hand.

Prepare glasses, fruit juices, fruit garnishes and ingredients like sugar syrup, lemon and lime juices and coconut cream in advance of your guests arriving.

Make sure that you have plenty of ice. A well-insulated, large-capacity ice bucket is better than a 'novelty' design. Tongs are more efficient than a spoon for taking ice from the bucket (this way, you won't get any unwanted water).

equipment

Some of the items that you'll find listed below will already be in your kitchen – and it is possible to improvise. (After all, necessity, they say, is the mother of invention!) You will need three basic pieces of equipment for making cocktails: a shaker, a mixing glass and a blender.

There are two types of shaker. The standard shaker has a built-in strainer, which is very convenient and easy to use, particularly for drinks made with such ingredients as eggs, cream, sugar syrup and fruit, which are shaken and strained to remove any bits of ice or fruit that may spoil the look of a drink. A Boston shaker consists of two flat-bottomed cones: one fits into the other and the liquid needs to be strained through a Hawthorn strainer, which is designed to fit over one of the cones.

A mixing glass is used for drinks that require stirring before they are poured, or strained, into the drinking glass. 'Professional' mixing glasses have been designed for use with a Hawthorn strainer, but you could use the bottom section of a standard shaker for straining. Alternatively, you could use a glass jug and could pour the drink through a fine-mesh sieve. Either method is fine.

A blender is ideal for making drinks with crushed ice, fresh fruits, ice cream and milk. When you blend a cocktail, the aim is to produce a drink with a milkshake-like consistency. Too much blending will

dilute the drink because crushed ice melts very quickly. You can also use a blender if you want to make up a large batch of drinks. (To serve a batch of the same drink, set the glasses in a row before you start. Fill each glass by half first, then back-track until the blender jug is empty. That way, everyone gets the same amount of drink, all thoroughly mixed.)

In addition, you will need:

a can- and bottle-opener/corkscrew;

a long-handled bar spoon;

a small, sharp paring knife for cutting fruit garnishes;

a measuring spoon for measuring 'dry' sugar;

a jigger, or your chosen measure;

an ice bucket and tongs;

assorted straws, swizzle sticks/stirrers, muddlers, cocktail

sticks/toothpicks with which to spear garnishes; glasses.

glasses

All of your glasses must be spotlessly clean! Test each type of glass to see how much it holds. This will allow you to adjust your measure and various quantities so that the final drink fits the glass perfectly.

Using the 'correct' glass adds to the visual impact of a drink, but different styles have been designed with particular spirits and drinks in mind: a brandy snifter is shaped so that the liquor is gently warmed by the hands; a champagne flute is designed to keep the bubbles in the glass; a straight-sided, pousse-café glass helps to create the separate layers, for

example. For each recipe, you will find the type of glass recommended for that particular drink and, where possible, an alternative suggestion. The type of glass is important to the drink, but the style and size of each type is a matter of personal taste.

Champagne saucer
This is the 'open', cup-shaped glass often seen in the movies. Because of the open shape, bubbles in the champagne are quickly dissipated, so it is more common for champagne and sparkling white wines to be served in flutes (see page 14). Nevertheless, because it is such an attractive glass, the champagne saucer has its place. It holds 150ml (5fl oz).

Cocktail glass
Elegant and stemmed to protect the chilled contents from the heat of a hand. Holds about 150ml (5fl oz). A double cocktail glass holds around 225ml (8fl oz).

Shot glass
This is the little glass used to serve 'shooters' and shots of ice-cold vodkas and akavits.

Rocks glass
Sometimes called an 'old-fashioned', or a tumbler, this is a short, chunky glass holding around 225ml (8fl oz).

Goblet
This is a large-bowled glass on a short stem that holds around 350ml (12fl oz). You can use a large wine glass or, indeed, any attractive, 'wide-mouthed' glass, like a poco or hurricane glass, since many of the drinks served in these glasses are rich and creamy.

Brandy snifter
This comes in sizes up to 3lcl (11fl oz). The balloon-shaped bowl on a short stem enables the cognac to be warmed by the drinker's hand, while the narrow mouth ensures that little of the spiritous vapours escapes.

Small wine glass
The rounded bowl on a fairly long stem is ideal for mixed drinks. Available in various styles and sizes, a good size is around 20cl (7fl oz).

Champagne flute
This is a tall, thin and stemmed glass – sometimes called a tulip – that holds around 150ml (5fl oz).

Hurricane
This glass is similar to the poco, the glass used for serving coladas, but is often a little more elongated.

Highball
A tall glass, normally holding around 225ml (8fl oz).

Collins glass
Narrow, very tall, often with straight sides and designed for long drinks. Typically holds about 300ml (10fl oz).

the well-stocked bar

The basis for many cocktails, no matter how exotic, remains a spirit. These are mixed with each other, with liqueurs, with fruit juices, with eggs, with cream and with coconut cream to produce thousands of exciting combinations. Look through the recipes and find the 'flavours' that interest you: then look at the ingredients to see what you need.

spirits

Gin

London dry gin is made from a distillate of unmalted grain. The spirit is infused with juniper and other 'botanicals' before and during distillation to produce a gin with a subtle flavour and aroma. London dry din is therefore a 'style' of gin, and there are many famous brands to choose from, such as Gordon's, Bombay Sapphire and Beefeater.

Plymouth gin is made only in Plymouth, England, and is the traditional gin used for a pink lady (see page 29).

Sloe gin – and its French equivalent, **prunelle** – is not a spirit, but a liqueur

made of sweetened gin in which the fruits (sloes) of the blackthorn bush have been steeped and then strained out, having stained the spirit a deep red.

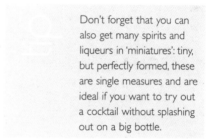

Don't forget that you can also get many spirits and liqueurs in 'miniatures': tiny, but perfectly formed, these are single measures and are ideal if you want to try out a cocktail without splashing out on a big bottle.

Tequila and mescal

Tequila is a spirit distilled in the region of the same name in Mexico, from the cactus-like plant *Agave tequilana*. The heart of the cactus is harvested, steam-cooked and crushed to remove the juice, which is then fermented and double-distilled. It is available as silver (blanco), which is colourless, and gold, which is a golden colour. **Mescal** is the juice or pulque of the agave cactus, which is distilled only once.

Vodka

Vodka is an almost neutral spirit distilled from a fermented mash of grain, which is filtered through charcoal. There are colourless and odourless varieties, as well as subtly flavoured and aromatised versions, including bison-grass vodka, cherry vodka, lemon vodka and pepper vodka.

Rum

Rum is the distilled spirit of fermented sugar-cane sap. The cane is crushed to remove the sap, the water is allowed to evaporate and the resulting syrup is spun in a centrifuge to separate the molasses, which are extracted, reduced by boiling, then fermented and distilled. The exceptions to this method are rums from Haiti and Martinique, which are made from reduced, but otherwise unprocessed, sugar-cane sap.

Dark rum is matured for about five years in barrels previously used for bourbon. The rum is then blended, and sometimes caramel (burnt sugar) is added to darken the colour.

White rum is a clear, colourless, light-bodied rum. The molasses are fermented, then distilled in a column-still to produce the clear spirit, which is aged for just one year before bottling.

Golden rum is produced in the same way as white rum, but is aged for around three years in charred barrels, which give the rum its golden hue and mellow flavour.

Whisky (Scotch & Canadian) or Whiskey (Irish, American & Japanese)

Malt whisky is made from barley, which has germinated, been dried over smoky peat fires, mashed, fermented, distilled and aged in wooden casks for 10 to 12 years or more.

Blended Scotch is a mixture of grain spirit – usually maize – and one or more malt whisky.

Bourbon is a generic term for a bourbon-style, American whiskey distilled in a continuous still method from fermented cereal mash containing a minimum of 51 per cent corn, and aged for 6 to 8 years in oak casks.

Canadian whisky is made from cereal grains, such as barley, corn, rye and wheat, in varying proportions depending on the manufacturer, in a continuous still method. It is aged for six years.

Irish whiskey is similar to Scotch, but the difference is that the barley is dried in a kiln rather than over a peat fire.

Rye whisky or whiskey is produced in both Canada and the United States, and is distilled from a mixture of cereals, but contains no less than 51 per cent rye.

Brandy and Cognac

Both brandy and Cognac are spirits made from distilled grape wine.
Brandy can be made in any country where vines are grown – pisco is a clear brandy from Peru and Chile – but **Cognac** can only come from the Cognac region in France, where it is made from white wines and distilled in traditional pot-stills before maturing in oak casks.

Cognacs are labelled VSO ('very superior old'), VSOP ('very superior old pale'), VVSOP ('very, very superior old pale') and XO ('extremely old').

Armagnac is a grape brandy produced in the Cognac region, in the south-west, of France and uses only specified white wines in three sectors: haut armagnac (white), Tenareze and bas armagnac (black). If the spirit is described simply as 'Armagnac', it is a blend of these three types.

Calvados and applejack

Calvados is an apple brandy made in Normandy, France.

Applejack is an American apple brandy, sometimes known as 'Jersey lightning' after the state in which it is produced. It is sold straight or blended with neutral spirits.

Eaux de vie *('waters of life')*

Eaux de vie are spirits produced from fruits other than grapes and apples. They are colourless (because they have not been aged in wooden casks) fruit brandies, most often made from soft berries, such as raspberries, strawberries, pears and cherries. Eaux de vie are not sweetened, and should not be confused with their syrupy liqueur cousins of the same flavours, which tend to be coloured.

Kirsch

Kirsch is the original 'cherry spirit' – a true brandy or eau de vie – made from cherries, and is normally regarded as a 'separate' product from other fruit brandies and eaux de vie. It is a particular speciality of Bavaria, in western Germany (*Kirsch* means 'cherry' in German). But remember, Kirsch is colourless, and is not related to the bright-red and sweet, syrupy 'cherry-brandy' liqueurs available.

Bitters

The term 'bitters' refers to a number of spirits flavoured with bitter herbs and roots. These range from products like **Campari**, which can be drunk in whole measures like any other spirit, or can be mixed with other ingredients, to bitters that are added in drops to 'season' a drink. The most famous of these 'dropping' bitters are **angostura bitters**, made from a secret Trinidadian recipe.

Akavit or aquavit

Akavit, or aquavit, is a grain and/or potato-based spirit that has been aromatised with fragrant spices or herbs, such as caraway seeds, fennel, cumin, dill and bitter oranges. The Scandinavian countries and Germany produce the true akavits, which are often called '**schnaps**' or '**schnapps**' – a name derived from the old Nordic word 'snappen', meaning 'to snatch or seize', which denotes the traditional way of drinking them: down in one gulp!

Liqueurs

Advocaat

Advocaat is a liqueur that originated in the Netherlands. It is made of a base spirit and sweetened egg yolks.

Amaretto

Amaretto is an almond-flavoured liqueur. The most famous brand is Disaronno Amaretto, but others are also available.

Anisette

Anisette is a French, sweetened and aniseed-flavoured liqueur, the most famous brand of which is Marie Brizard.

Irish cream

Irish cream is a sweet, cream liqueur (as distinct from a crème liqueur, see below) made with whiskey and cream and flavoured with coffee. **Baileys** is the best-known proprietary brand.

Benedictine

Benedictine is a bright, golden and aged liqueur made from a secret recipe and comprising seventy-five herbs.

Chartreuse

Chartreuse is a French liqueur made by monks. There are two colours: green, which is intensely powerful and aromatic, and yellow Chartreuse, which is sweeter and has a slightly minty flavour.

Coconut rum

Coconut rum is a sweet, white-rum-based liqueur flavoured with coconut. The best-known proprietary brand is **Malibu**.

Crème liqueurs

Crème liqueurs are sweetened liqueurs – as distinct from dry spirits like whisky or Cognac – and consist of one dominant flavour, which is often fruit. There are also nut-flavoured liqueurs.

Crème de banane: a sweet, clear, yellow, banana liqueur.

A banana liqueur made from green bananas is pisang ambon, from Indonesia.

Crème de cacao: a chocolate-flavoured liqueur, available as dark and light, which has a more subtle flavour and is colourless because the cocoa remains are absent.

Crème de cassis: a blackcurrant-flavoured liqueur.

Crème de menthe: white and green liqueurs distilled from a concentrate of mint leaves. The white version has a more subtle taste than the green, which gets its colour from an added colorant.

Crème de fraise: a strawberry-flavoured liqueur.

Crème de framboise: a raspberry-flavoured liqueur.

Curaçao

Curaçao was originally a white-rum-based liqueur flavoured with the peel of bitter, green oranges from the island of Curaçao. Today, it is made by a number of companies, with brandy as the base spirit. Cointreau, Grand Marnier and Mandarine Napoleon are all forms of Curaçao. A variant name was 'triple sec' (the most famous being Cointreau), but confusingly, Curaçao is not sec (dry), but always sweet. Curaçao comes in a range of colours, as well as a clear version: orange, red, yellow, green and blue. Whatever the colour, they all taste of orange, and they do add a wonderful colour to mixed drinks and cocktails.

Galliano

Galliano is a golden-yellow liqueur from Italy, made to a secret recipe of some eighty herbs, roots and berries, with the principal flavourings being liquorice, anise and vanilla.

Kahlua and Tia Maria

Kahlua and Tia Maria are dark-brown, coffee-flavoured liqueurs from Mexico (Kahlua) and Jamaica (Tia Maria).

Kümmel

Kümmel is a pure-grain distillate – effectively a type of vodka – in which caraway seeds are infused to produce a spearmint-flavoured liqueur made in Latvia, Poland, Germany, Denmark, the Netherlands and the United States.

Liqueur brandies

There are essentially three fruit liqueur brandies: cherry, apricot and peach (although this last is not often seen). These are not 'true' brandies, but sweetened and coloured liqueurs based on a simple grape brandy that has been flavoured with the relevant fruit, as opposed to being distillates of the fruit itself.

Maraschino

Maraschino is a clear, colourless liqueur derived from an infusion of pressed cherries and cherrystone distillate and aged for several years. Originally, marasca cherries grown in Dalmatia were used, but when this area became part of the Venetian 'empire', plantings of the marasca-cherry trees were established in the Veneto.

Melon liqueur

Melon liqueur is a bright-green, sweet and syrupy liqueur, the most famous being the Japanese brand **Midori**, first devised in the 1980s.

Pastis

Pastis is a traditional drink of the Mediterranean countries, from Spain to Greece and beyond, where it is known by a variety of names. The principal flavouring agent is either liquorice or aniseed, along with other herbal ingredients, which are steeped in a neutral alcohol base. 'Pastis' is an old French word meaning 'pastiche', 'a mixture' or 'a muddle'. **Pernod** and **Ricard** are the best-known brands. Greece has **ouzo**, while **Sambuca** is an Italian, aniseed-flavoured liqueur made from anise, herbs and roots.

Southern Comfort

America's foremost liqueur is Southern Comfort, which uses American whiskey and peaches in a recipe that is a closely guarded secret. The practice of blending peach juice and whiskey was common in the bars of the southern states of America during the 19th century. Unusually, for a liqueur, Southern Comfort has a high bottled strength – 40 per cent alcohol by volume (abv).

Wines and fortified wines

Fortified wines are wines that have been strengthened by the addition of a spirit – usually a grape spirit. The world's classic fortified wines, such as **Madeira**, **Marsala**, **muscat** and **muscatel**, each has its own method of production, and the majority are made from white grapes. The most notable exception is **port**. **Sherry** contains only wine and grape spirit, but vermouth and related products contain a number of aromatising ingredients.

Vermouth

The cocktail bar would be nothing without vermouth. There are French vermouths and Italian vermouths; there are dry and sweet vermouths; and there are white, or 'bianco', rosé, and red, 'rosso' vermouths.

Champagne

The only wine used in this book, true champagne must be made by the champagne method, where the sparkle is made through secondary fermentation in the bottle, and not in a vat or by artificially carbonating it. To be called champagne, it must have been made using the prescribed method and been produced in the Champagne region of France, a region about 160km (100 miles) north-east of Paris, around the towns of Rheims and Epernay.

Juices and mixers

A well-stocked bar needs fresh fruit juices and such mixers as cola, lemonade, ginger ale, tonic and soda water, as well as lemon (and lime) juice, grenadine and a simple sugar syrup, sometimes called gomme syrup.

Grenadine is a sweet syrup flavoured with pomegranate juice, which gives it a rich, pink colour. It is used to add colour, flavour and sweetness to many cocktails. Once the bottle is open, the syrup will begin to ferment and go mouldy. Keep it in a cool place, but not in the fridge as this can cause the sugar to crystallise or harden, and this will stop it from mixing easily with other ingredients.

A number of drinks call for sweetening to offset the tartness of some juices. Granulated sugar doesn't dissolve that easily in cold solutions, so a sugar, or gomme, syrup – both liquid and colourless – is a simple, but effective alternative. To make a sugar or gomme syrup, dissolve equal volumes of water and sugar – say one cup of each – and simmer the liquid over a very low heat in a saucepan until all of the sugar has dissolved. You may need to skim the syrup to make it clear. Allow the syrup to cool and then decant it into a handy sized bottle that pours well and store it in a cool place.

To make coconut cream, take a hard block of chilled, pure, creamed coconut and grate it up to break down the grainy texture. Use 1 tablespoon of the grated coconut cream with slightly less than 1 tablespoon of powdered/caster sugar (you can adjust the sweetness to suit your own taste) and mix them together with the absolute minimum of hot water. Stir until you have a smooth, creamy paste that is slightly runny, but coats the back of a spoon. When it's cool, it's ready for use. Use it the same day (if you try to store it, the cream will separate, become grainy or turn rancid).

one last word

Before you start, please stop and consider the following: the cocktails in this book are for adults, and should be drunk in moderation.

- Responsible drinking is the key to enjoyment, health and safety – both yours and that of others – especially if you are a driver. Do not drink and drive, and never offer 'one for the road'.

- Do not condone or encourage under-age drinking. There are numerous non-alcoholic, 'fruity' syrups that can be used to create delicious 'mocktails'. You will find that these are very popular with many people because they are so tasty. Be prepared, when you entertain, to cater for all of your guests.

- Do not push an alcoholic drink on to a guest.

- Never, ever, spike anyone's drink: they may be the designated driver that night, be allergic to alcohol, be on medication, have religious beliefs that preclude alcohol, or they may be 'in recovery'.

garnishes

Some cocktails and mixed drinks are served with fruit garnishes, straws or stirrers. A traditional garnish is given for each recipe.

gin cocktails

Gin and tonic is considered a quintessentially English mix, but it was in Holland that the original gin – a rye spirit flavoured with juniper – developed. The English had their first taste of the spirit in the 16th century: in 1585, English mercenaries arrived in the Low Countries to help the Dutch fight their Spanish overlord, King Philip II. When the soldiers returned home, they brought gin with them and it was distilled in England as 'geneva'.

In the 17th century, Dutch influence in England was further strengthened when William of Orange became king of Great Britain and Ireland in 1689. When Britain went to war with France, William raised the import duty on brandy and gave everyone in England the right to distil spirits. Gin thus began to develop its English identity.

At the heart of gin is a neutral, grain spirit that is redistilled with what are called 'botanicals': a range of herbs, spices and fruits that, depending on the recipe, includes juniper, coriander, angelica, ginger, nutmeg, lemon and orange peel, almonds, cassia bark, cinnamon and liquorice root. The alcoholic strength of the gin influences the flavour imparted by the botanicals: the stronger the gin, the more intense their flavour. Plymouth gin, made with water from Devon, and the gin favoured for pink gin, is available at a hefty 57 per cent alcohol by volume (abv). London gin is a particular style of dry gin at 37.5 per cent abv. Sloe gin is not a true gin, but rather a liqueur. It is made by macerating sloes – the small, dark fruit of the blackthorn – in gin.

Larios is a Spanish gin that has been made since 1863, while in the Netherlands, there are three main styles of genever based on wheat, rye, maize and malted barley: young genever, old genever and korenwijn. The difference between young and old genevers is not their age, but the difference in recipes: old genever is made to the traditional recipe, and is a slightly sweeter, more aromatic, straw-coloured spirit than the clear, young genever. Korenwijn is made of the finest-quality grain distillates, which are then aged in oak barrels. Bols' korenwijn is matured for three years and is then bottled in the famous, handmade, 'stone' jars.

Gin is one of the most common base spirits for cocktails, including the most famous cocktail of them all, the martini. The reason why so many cocktails of the Prohibition era were devised was because the only gin available was bathtub gin. Concocted illegally in a bathtub, this bootleg gin bore little, if any, relation to the premium gins available outside of America, and would have been pretty unpleasant drunk neat. By disguising its rawness with bitters, juices and other spirits and liqueurs, however, even the crudest bathtub gin was found to be a versatile spirit.

martini

Dry martini

6 to 8 ice cubes

I measure gin

I measure dry vermouth

I green olive, to garnish

Medium martini

6 to 8 ice cubes

I measure gin

I measure dry vermouth

I measure sweet vermouth

Sweet martini

6 to 8 ice cubes

I measure gin

I measure sweet vermouth

I cocktail cherry, to garnish

There are as many variations of the martini as there are bartenders. All have their own, favourite recipe, but in general, the difference lies in the degree of sweetness imparted by the vermouth and the garnish. The following recipes range from dry through medium to sweet. All are made using the same method stirred, never shaken!
The picture shows a dry martini.

Place 6 to 8 ice cubes in a mixing glass and pour on the gin and vermouth. Stir – some say 12 times, some say 20 times, you decide. Then strain into a well-chilled cocktail glass and garnish as appropriate.

alexander's sister

method: shaker   **glass:** cocktail   **ice:** cubes

Big brother Alexander is made with brandy (see page 119), while his little sister – who can pack a punch or two herself – is a gin-based, creamy and minty cocktail. The mint flavour and the pale, eau-de-nil colour come from the green crème de menthe, a sweet liqueur distilled from various types of mint.

ingredients

3 to 4 ice cubes
$^3/_4$ measure gin
$^3/_4$ measure green crème de menthe
$^3/_4$ measure double cream

method

Drop the ice into a shaker and add all of the ingredients. Shake firmly and then strain into a cocktail glass.

suzy wong

Emperor Napoleon is said to have wooed his favourite actress with a citrus-flavoured liqueur. This fruity, yet dry, cocktail makes use of both gin and Mandarine Napoleon, a form of Curacao. The liqueur is made in Belgium by macerating Andalusian tangerines in aged Cognac.

1 wedge of lemon

caster sugar, for rimming

6 to 8 ice cubes

3/4 measure lemon juice

3/4 measure gin

3/4 measure Mandarine Napoleon

chilled champagne or sparkling white wine, to top up

1/2 slice of orange, to garnish

Run a wedge of lemon around the rim of a champagne saucer and dip the glass into caster sugar. Place plenty of ice in a shaker and add all of the ingredients except for the champagne or sparkling wine and orange garnish. Shake well and strain into the champagne saucer. Top with chilled champagne or wine and garnish with the 1/2 slice of orange.

empire

method: mixing glass   **glass:** cocktail   **ice:** cubes   **garnish:** maraschino cherry

The 1930s were not only the heyday of the cocktail, but of that most modern symbol of urban life, the skyscraper. New York's famous Empire State Building, designed by the architects Shrev, Lamb and Harmon, was constructed between 1930 and 1933. From its observation decks, visitors can look out across the city and marvel at a skyline that is pierced by such architectural gems and monuments to business empires as the Chrysler and Woolworth buildings.

ingredients

6 to 8 ice cubes

1 measure gin

$1/2$ measure Calvados or applejack

$1/2$ measure apricot brandy

1 maraschino cherry, to garnish

method

Place plenty of ice in a mixing glass and add all of the ingredients except for the cherry garnish. Strain into a cocktail glass and garnish with a maraschino cherry.

pogo stick

method: shaker **glass:** highball or collins **ice:** cubes **garnish:** ½ slice grapefruit

The pogo stick, like the cocktail, was a craze of the 'roaring twenties'. It was invented and patented by George Harsburg in 1919, and soon everyone was bouncing. Harburg taught the Ziegfeld Follies to pogo, and the chorus girls of the New York Hippodrome even performed an entire show on pogo sticks.

6 to 8 ice cubes

2 measures grapefruit juice

2 tsps lemon juice

1 measure gin

³/₄ measure Cointreau

¹/₂ slice grapefruit, to garnish

Place plenty of ice in a shaker and add all of the ingredients except for the grapefruit garnish. Shake and strain into a highball or collins glass half-filled with ice cubes. Garnish with the ¹/₂ slice of grapefruit.

chihuahua bite

method: shaker   **glass:** cocktail   **ice:** cubes   **garnish:** twist of lemon

The Mexican state of Chihuahua is named after its capital city. The exact origins of the name are not known, although it is thought to derive from *Xicuahua*, which means 'dry, sandy place'. Although most associated with the breed of small dog that bears the same name, Chihuahua is also home to something much bigger: the Barranca del Cobre, or Copper Canyon, a spectacular canyon system that rivals America's Grand Canyon.

ingredients

3 to 4 ice cubes

1 measure lime cordial

3 measures gin

1 measure Calvados or applejack

thin strip of lemon peel, to garnish

method

Drop the ice into a shaker and add all of the ingredients except for the lemon peel. Shake well and strain into a cocktail glass. Twist the lemon rind over the glass to release its oil and then drop it into the drink.

pink lady

method: shaker   **glass:** champagne saucer or cocktail   **ice:** cubes

There are a number of variations of the 'lady', ranging from white through pink to blue! The original pink lady was devised in 1912, and was named after a popular Broadway show. Originally, it used cream, as well as egg white.

grenadine, for rimming

caster sugar, for rimming

2 to 3 ice cubes

1$^1/_2$ measures Plymouth gin

$^1/_2$ the white of a small egg

$^1/_3$ measure grenadine

$^3/_4$ measure lemon juice

Rim a champagne saucer or cocktail glass with a little grenadine and then dip it into caster sugar. Place the ice in a shaker and add all of the remaining ingredients. Shake well and strain into the glass.

lemon flip

Flips take their name from the method of flipping them over and over between two vessels to obtain a smooth mix. They first became popular during the 1690s, when they were made of beaten eggs, sugar, spices, rum and hot ale. Today, however, they are served short and cold, but still contain egg yolk. Don't be put off: the egg in this refreshing mix is effectively 'cooked' by the gin and Cointreau.

ingredients

3 to 4 ice cubes

1½ measures lemon juice

1 measure gin

¾ measure Cointreau

1 yolk of a small egg

½ slice lemon, to garnish

method

Place the ice in a shaker and add all of the ingredients except for the lemon garnish. Shake firmly, strain into a champagne flute and garnish with the ½ slice of lemon.

blue lady

The original 'lady' was white, a mix of crème de menthe and Cointreau or Curaçao. In 1929, Harry MacElhone replaced the mint with gin and created a very popular cocktail. This version uses blue Curaçao, but it still tastes of oranges. If you prefer your mix a little sweeter, adjust the amount of lemon juice to suit your taste.

I wedge of lemon

caster sugar, for rimming

3 to 4 ice cubes

I measure lemon juice

I measure gin

I measure blue Curaçao

I maraschino cherry , to garnish

Run a wedge of lemon around the rim of a well-chilled cocktail glass and dip the glass into caster sugar. Place the ice in a shaker and pour on the lemon juice, gin and blue Curaçao. Shake well and strain into the cocktail glass. Garnish with a maraschino cherry.

the original *singapore sling*

method: mixing glass   **glass:** highball   **ice:** broken   **garnish:** pineapple slice & maraschino cherry

The world-famous Singapore sling was devised at the Raffles Hotel, in Singapore, in 1915, by Ngiam Tong Boon. It was originally intended as a lady's drink, but it soon became widely enjoyed by both sexes. It was the favourite drink of the writers Somerset Maugham and Joseph Conrad, and of the Hollywood actor Douglas Fairbanks. Some modern interpretations use soda water to finish the drink, but in this, the Raffles Hotel Bar version, it is never used.

ingredients

3 to 4 ice cubes

1 measure gin

1 measure cherry brandy

$1/2$ measure Cointreau

1 measure lime juice

1 measure pineapple juice

1 measure orange juice

$1/4$ measure grenadine

1 dash angostura bitters

1 tsp Benedictine

1 slice pineapple, to garnish

1 maraschino cherry, to garnish

method

Place the ice cubes and all of the ingredients except the Benedictine and garnishes in a shaker and shake well. Strain into a highball glass three-quarters filled with broken ice and sprinkle the Benedictine on top. Garnish with the slice of pineapple and the maraschino cherry and serve with straws.

million-dollar cocktail

Like the Singapore sling (see page 37), this cocktail was created by Ngiam Tong Boon, barman *extraordinaire* at the Raffles Hotel in Singapore. In spite of its name, the ingredients used are not the most luxurious or expensive. As a popular song of the 1930s said, 'I found a million-dollar baby at a five-and-ten-cent store'!

ingredients

3 to 4 ice cubes

1 measure gin

¼ measure sweet vermouth

¼ measure dry vermouth

4 measures pineapple juice

dash egg white

dash angostura bitters

method

Place all of the ingredients in a shaker and shake well to froth up the egg white. Strain into a highball or collins glass (over ice, if you like).

blue arrow

method: shaker   **glass:** cocktail   **ice:** crushed

A gorgeous, blue drink that is a smash hit at parties. The citrus flavours of the Cointreau, lime cordial and blue Curaçao, alongside that of that cocktail stalwart, gin, make for a winning combination, while the blue arrow's colour has been described as being like the Mediterranean on a hot summer's day.

ingredients

1 good scoop crushed ice

2 measures gin

1 measure Cointreau

1 measure lime cordial

1 measure blue Curaçao

method

Place all of the ingredients in a shaker and shake vigorously for about 5 seconds. Strain into a well-chilled cocktail glass.

tom collins

This drink is often called a John Collins (the original Collins was indeed John, the head waiter at Limmers Hotel in London during the 18th century). The original recipe used a heavy, Dutch-style gin, which was not popular in America. A London gin called Old Tom proved more successful there, hence the cocktail's name.

1 measure London dry gin

1 dash sugar syrup

juice of 1 lemon

chilled soda water

Half-fill a highball or collins glass with ice and pour over the gin, sugar syrup and lemon juice. Stir gently, top up with chilled soda water and then garnish with the lemon slice.

You can make a Collins with your favourite spirit: Pierre Collins with Cognac; Mike Collins with Irish whiskey; Jack Collins with Calvados or applejack; Pedro Collins with rum; and Juan Collins with tequila!

wedding belle

method: shaker   **glass:** cocktail   **ice:** crushed

In recent years, cocktails have been enjoying something of a revival, and new styles of mixed drinks now complement the cocktail classics. This delicious mix uses Dubonnet, one of the best-known French apéritifs, whose flavur is like a good marriage: the first taste is sweet, and it soon becomes very smooth! Try this lovely cocktail to toast a beautiful bride with on her special day.

ingredients

1 good scoop crushed ice

1 measure gin

1 measure Dubonnet

1/2 measure cherry brandy

1 measure orange juice

method

Place all of the ingredients in a shaker and shake well. Strain into a chilled cocktail glass.

royal fizz

method: mixing glass   **glass:** highball or collins   **ice:** cubes

Fizzes first came to light during the 1890s. They are similar to a Collins, but are always shaken before soda or sparkling mineral water is added, and only use half a glass of ice to ensure that the soda effervesces. During the late 19th and early 20th centuries, fizzes were served in the morning or at midday as a pick-me-up.

ingredients

6 to 8 ice cubes

1 1/2 measures gin

3/4 measure lemon juice

2 tsps sugar syrup

1 egg

chilled soda water, for topping up

method

Place 3 to 4 ice cubes and all of the remaining ingredients except for the soda water in a shaker and shake vigourously. Strain and pour into a highball or collins glass half-filled with the remaining ice cubes and top up with soda water.

You can also have a silver fizz: instead of using the whole egg, use just the egg white.

barfly's dream

method: shaker   **glass:** cocktail   **ice:** cubes

'A barfly' was once American slang for someone who frequented bars, and probably implied a drunk! Today, being a barfly is taken very seriously: there is even an international association of barflies, the members of which are identified by their distinctive lapel pin, showing a fly on a sugar cube. The serious task of tasting cocktails and mixed drinks falls to these 'bibbers'. This spicy mix must have been a 'dream come true' for them!

ingredients

3 to 4 ice cubes

1 measure gin

1 measure dark rum

1 measure pineapple juice

method

Place all of the ingredients in a shaker and shake well. Strain into a cocktail glass.

take five

The expression 'take five' probably has its origins among the jazz musicians of the Prohibition-era speakeasy, when it meant a five-minute break between sets. Later in the 20th century, jazz composer Dave Brubeck made it the title of a memorable piece of music that's still as cool and laid-back as this drink.

3 to 4 ice cubes

1 measure gin

1 measure lemon juice

³/₄ measure sugar syrup

2 tsps orange juice

2 tsps grenadine

1 slice lime, to garnish

Shake all of the ingredients except for the lime garnish in a shaker. Strain into a chilled cocktail glass and garnish with the slice of lime.

tequila cocktails

Said to have been first made by the Aztecs, who are rumoured to have made the pulque (the fermented juice of the agave) after seeing one of the plants being struck by lightening, it was the Spanish who discovered that this fermented pulque could be made even stronger by distilling it into a spirit. It took a long time for tequila to move across the border into the United States: the first-recorded shipment was in 1873. Later, three barrels were taken home from Mexico by American troops in 1916, following battles with the staunchly teetotal Pancho Villa. Tequila most likely crossed the border during the Prohibition, but it was not until the 1950s that the drink developed something of a cult following. While many content themselves with the suck-a-lime, knock-back-tequila, lick-salt routine of the tequila slammer, enterprising and imaginative bartenders have put tequila to new uses in cocktails and mixed drinks.

Tequila, Mexico's number-one spirit, is a distillation from a plant: the blue agave, of which 51 per cent of the product must consist by law. (The remaining 49 per cent is made up of cane or other types of sugar.) *Agave tequilana*, a cactus-like plant, is, in fact, a member of the lily family. The bulbous heart of the agave is harvested after eight to ten years' growth, the leaves are removed and the heart is then steam-cooked and crushed. The resulting juice is fermented and distilled in pot stills to make the spirit.

Clear, white tequila, which is also known as silver tequila, is matured for a very short period in stainless-steel or wax-lined vats, which is why it is colourless. (Some lesser brands of white tequila are coloured with caramel to suggest age.) Gold tequila, on the other hand, gets both its name and its colour from maturing in oak vats. Gold tequila labelled 'Reposado' has been matured in oak tanks for up to six months, while 'Anejo' has been kept for at least one year – and often two or three, and occasionally eight to ten, years – in oak barrels previously used to store bourbon.

Mexican law stipulates that only tequila produced in a specific geographical area around the town of Tequila can be labelled as such. Mescal is a similar drink, distilled from a different variety of agave, but its production is not as tightly controlled, and it does not have the same labelling regulations. It is mescal – and not tequila – that traditionally contains a pickled worm at the bottom of the bottle.

mexican dream

method: shaker   **glass:** cocktail   **ice:** cubes   **garnish:** lemon twist

This is a very tangy, fruity cocktail, combining tequila and brandy. For a truly south-of-the-border mix, try pisco, a clear brandy made in Peru and Chile from the remains of fermented muscat grapes following their pressing for wine production.

ingredients

3 to 4 ice cubes

³/₄ measure tequila

³/₄ measure pisco (or brandy)

³/₄ measure lemon juice

thin strip of lemon peel,
to garnish

method

Shake all of the ingredients together in a shaker and strain into a cocktail glass. Squeeze the lemon peel over the glass, to release the oil, and then drop it into the drink.

mexican mockingbird

method: shaker   **glass:** highball or collins   **ice:** cubes   **garnish:** mint sprig

This long, refreshing drink is related to the fizzes of the late 19th century, but uses tequila. While some liqueurs, such as Benedictine and Chartreuse, have long been made by holy men on Earth, tequila, according to Aztec legend, was first made by the gods, when they fired a bolt of lighting at an agave plant.

ingredients

6 to 8 ice cubes

1 1/2 measures tequila

3/4 measure green crème de menthe

2 tsps lime juice

chilled soda water, as required

1 mint sprig, to garnish

method

Place all of the ingredients except for the soda water and mint sprig in a shaker. Shake and then strain into a tall glass half-filled with ice. Top with chilled soda water and stir briefly. Garnish with the sprig of mint.

midori margarita

method: shaker **glass:** champagne saucer **ice:** cubes **garnish:** lime wedge

The actress Marjorie King was the inspiration behind the original margarita, created back in 1948 at Rancho del Gloria, Danny Herrera's restaurant near Tijuana, New Mexico. Today, there are dozens of variations, including the blue margarita, the Galliano margarita and the golden margarita. There are also frozen-fruit margaritas, which are served over crushed ice. What they all have in common is tequila and the famously salted (or sugared) rim of the glass. This variation uses Midori, a vibrant-green, melon liqueur from Japan.

lemon juice, for rimming

salt, for rimming

3 to 4 ice cubes

1 measure white or silver tequila

1 tbsp lime juice

1 measure Midori

1 wedge of lime, to garnish

Chill a champagne saucer. Moisten the rim with the lemon juice and dip it into the salt. Put the ice in a shaker and pour in the tequila, lime juice and Midori. Shake and then strain into the salt-rimmed glass and garnish with a wedge of lime.

harvey floor-walker

method: build   **glass:** highball or collins   **ice:** cubes

The drinks' world is home to a number of Harveys. First, there is the firm of Harvey's of Bristol, famous for shipping the fine, oloroso sherry that bears the name Harvey's Bristol Cream. Second, there's Harvey, the Californian surfer whose nickname was Harvey Wallbanger. This, more recent, tequila-and-rum mix is the creation of Reece Clark, of the Fifth Floor Bar at London's Harvey Nichols department store.

ingredients

3 to 4 ice cubes

1½ measures gold tequila

¾ measure gold rum

1 tbsp blue Curaçao

1½ measures chilled orange juice

method

Put a few ice cubes into a tall highball or collins glass and pour on the tequila, rum and blue Curaçao. Gently pour on the chilled orange juice.

icebreaker

method: blender   **glass:** rocks   **ice:** crushed

This refreshingly fruity drink is a little like a daiquiri (see page 82), and a little like a frozen margarita. The sweetness of the Cointreau is nicely offset here by the grapefruit juice. You'll need a blender if you want to make this drink, but it's well worth the preparation.

ingredients

2 good scoops crushed ice

2 measures tequila

2 tsps Cointreau

2 measures grapefruit juice

1 tbsp grenadine

method

Put the crushed ice in a blender and pour in the tequila, Cointreau, grapefruit juice and grenadine. Mix at the lowest speed for 15 seconds, then strain into a rocks glass and drink straight up.

frozen matador

method: blender   **glass:** rocks   **ice:** crushed   **garnish:** pineapple slice & mint leaves

This frothy, frozen mix is reminiscent of the refreshing drinks available from street vendors in Mexico, who sell a huge range of fruit juices (*jugos*), iced 'shakes' (*liquados*) and flavoured waters (*aquas frescas*). This simple mix of crushed ice, tequila and pineapple juice is easy to prepare in quantity in a blender and makes a great drink for long, hot summer days.

ingredients

2 good scoops crushed ice

dash of lime juice

1 measure pineapple juice

1 measure tequila

2 ice cubes

1 slice pineapple, to garnish

2 to 3 mint leaves, to garnish

method

Place the crushed ice in a blender and pour in the lime juice, pineapple juice and tequila. Blend to a frothy mix and strain into a rocks glass over 2 ice cubes. Garnish with the slice of pineapple and mint leaves.

earthquake

method: blender   **glass:** cocktail   **ice:** crushed   **garnish:** 2 strawberries & orange slice

Tequila thrives in variations on the theme of the margarita, created in 1948 by Danny Herrera for the actress Marjorie King. This glorious, frozen, pink version forsakes the more usual, salted, rimmed glass and opts for not one, but two strawberries. It's easy to prepare in a blender – and in quantity – so it makes a perfect party drink.

2 good scoops crushed ice

1¹/₂ measures tequila

1 tsp grenadine

2 dashes of Cointreau

2 strawberries, to garnish

1 slice of orange, to garnish

Put the crushed ice in a blender and pour in the tequila, grenadine and Cointreau. Mix at high speed for 15 seconds and then strain into a cocktail glass. Garnish with 2 strawberries and a slice of orange.

acapulco

method: shaker   **glass:** cocktail   **ice:** cubes   **garnish:** orange slice & maraschino cherry

A coconut-and-coffee-flavoured cocktail named after the internationally famous Mexican resort, this drink uses Mexico's other famous beverage, the coffee-flavoured liqueur Kahlua, and coconut cream. The coconut cream is very easy to make (see page 21).

ingredients

3 to 4 ice cubes

1 measure gold tequila

1 measure Kahlua

$^2/_3$ measure dark rum

$^1/_2$ measure coconut cream

1 slice orange, to garnish

1 maraschino cherry, to garnish

method

Shake all of the ingredients together firmly in a shaker, then strain into a cocktail glass. Garnish with a slice of orange and a maraschino cherry.

carabinieri

method: shaker   **glass:** collins   **ice:** crushed   **garnish:** lime slice, 1 red & 1 green maraschino cherry

This gorgeous cocktail hails from Canada, and is the creation of Francisco Pedroche, of the Hyatt Regency Hotel, Toronto. It combines a little bit of the Old World with the New World.

3 to 4 ice cubes

1 measure tequila

³/₄ measure Galliano

¹/₂ measure Cointreau

1 tsp lime cordial

1 egg yolk

1 slice lime, to garnish

1 red and 1 green maraschino cherry, to garnish

1 scoop crushed ice

Put some ice cubes in a shaker and pour on the remaining ingredients, except for the lime and cherry garnishes and the crushed ice. Shake well and then strain into a collins glass over crushed ice. Garnish with the lime slice and the cherries.

buttock-clencher

method: shaker   **glass:** highball   **ice:** cubes   **garnish:** pineapple cube & maraschino cherry

Many modern cocktails often appear to have outrageous, or rather suggestive, names. But many of the classic cocktails that date from the 1920s and 1930s have names that were equally outrageous at the time: the mere mention of a 'maiden's kiss' or 'between the sheets' would have brought a blush to many a cheek! In New York, during the 1930s, the famous French creation, the bloody Mary, was known as a 'red snapper' for a while because the original name was considered offensive!

ingredients

6 to 8 ice cubes

1 measure silver tequila

1 measure gin

¼ measure melon liqueur

2 measures pineapple juice

2 measures chilled lemonade

1 pineapple cube, to garnish

1 maraschino cherry, to garnish

method

Put 3 to 4 ice cubes in a shaker and pour on the tequila, gin, melon liqueur and pineapple juice. Shake well and strain into a tall highball glass half-filled with ice. Top with the chilled lemonade and garnish with a pineapple cube and maraschino cherry on a cocktail stick.

ridley

method: mixing glass   **glass:** champagne saucer   **ice:** crushed   **garnish:** orange slice & maraschino cherry

This subtle, aniseed-flavoured cocktail was created in 1960 at Dukes Hotel, London. The aniseed flavour – with just a hint of vanilla – is courtesy of Galliano, a golden-yellow liqueur from Lombardy, in Italy. It is named after a certain Major Giuseppe Galliano, who was forced to surrender after a 44-day siege of Fort Enda, during the Italian campaign to conquer Abyssinia (Ethiopia), in North Africa, during the 1890s. The event is depicted on the label of the tall bottle.

3 to 4 ice cubes

1 measure gold tequila

1 measure gin

1 scoop crushed ice

1 tsp Galliano

1 slice orange, to garnish

1 maraschino cherry, to garnish

Place the ice cubes in a mixing glass and add the tequila and gin. Stir well and strain into a champagne saucer filled with crushed ice. Sprinkle the Galliano on top. Garnish with a slice of orange and perch the maraschino cherry on the rim of the glass.

toreador

While the gods of the Old World feasted on ambrosia and nectar – fruit juice that probably never fermented into alcohol – the Aztec gods of the New World partied on tequila and chocolate! Fortunately, we mere mortals can join the party! This creamy confection makes a wonderful (adult) alternative to dessert.

ingredients

3 to 4 ice cubes

1 measure tequila

2 tsps brown crème de cacao

2 tsps single cream

1 good scoop whipped cream, to garnish

cocoa powder, for dusting

method

Put the ice in a shaker, add the tequila, brown crème de cacao and single cream and shake firmly. Strain into a cocktail glass, pile lashings of whipped cream on the top and dust generously with cocoa powder.

la conga

method: build   **glass:** rocks   **ice:** cubes   **garnish:** lemon slice

Although Mexican tequila is the base spirit for this drink, the conga dance is itself a native of Cuba. Composed of three steps forward and then a kick to the side, its simplicity – even the most inebriated party-goer can perform it – has ensured its success. This fruity and sharp, long and refreshing drink offers the perfect way to chill out.

6 to 8 ice cubes

2 tsps pineapple juice

2 dashes angostura bitters

1½ measures tequila

chilled soda water, as required

1 slice lemon, to garnish

Half-fill a rocks glass with ice cubes and pour in the pineapple juice, bitters and tequila. Stir gently, then pour on the soda water to top up the level and garnish with a slice of lemon.

golden volcano

method: shaker **glass:** cocktail **ice:** cubes **garnish:** maraschino cherry

Tequila is made near Guadalajara, in the Jalisco province of Mexico, principally in the town at the foot of the – happily dormant – volcano of the same name. It's not surprising, then, that award-winning cocktail barman Max Davies should have created a drink that makes reference to tequila's volcanic origins.

ingredients

3 to 4 ice cubes

2 tsps lime juice

2 tsps orange juice

1 tsp triple sec

2 tsps single cream

1/2 measure tequila

1/2 measure Galliano

1 maraschino cherry, to garnish

method

Put the ice cubes in a shaker and pour in the lime juice, orange juice, triple sec, cream and tequila and then the Galliano. Shake firmly and then strain into a cocktail glass. Garnish by perching a maraschino cherry on the rim.

tornado

There are a number of variations on the tornado theme among cocktails. Like the rotating winds, no two are the same, and some are more devastating than others. (One version includes schnaps in the mix!) This tequila-and-chocolate version may seem harmless at first, but prepare for the stormy weather to come, especially if you dare have one too many!

ingredients

3 to 4 ice cubes

2 measures silver tequila

1 measure white crème de cacao

1 measure double cream

grated chocolate, to garnish

method

Drop the ice into a shaker and add all of the remaining ingredients except for the grated chocolate. Shake firmly, then strain into a champagne saucer and sprinkle with grated chocolate – assuming that you haven't already eaten it all!

last chance

method: shaker   **glass:** rocks   **ice:** broken   **garnish:** lime wedge

The citrus flavour and sharpness of the lime and tequila are balanced perfectly here by the honey and apricot brandy – not true brandy (i.e., distilled from the fruit), but a fruit liqueur made by infusing fruit in a spirit base, which is usually brandy.

ingredients

2 good scoops broken ice

1³/₄ measures gold tequila

¹/₄ measure apricot brandy

1 measure lime juice

1 tsp honey

1 lime wedge, to garnish

method

Fill a shaker with broken ice and add all of the remaining ingredients, apart from the lime garnish. Shake well and pour, unstrained, into a rocks glass. Drop in the lime wedge.

vodka cocktails

Pure vodka is a clear, colourless and smooth spirit with a neutral taste. It is distilled from mixtures of grains, primarily wheat or barley (in Russia, Sweden and Finland), and sometimes rye. In Poland, potatoes are also distilled to produce Luksusowa and Cracovia vodkas. Beyond the Slav regions, other vodkas are made from a variety of raw materials, which range from beet in Turkey to molasses in Britain.

Vodka is the world's strongest commercially marketed spirit, originally produced by the Slavs in a bid to find a very strong spirit that would not freeze in extreme weather (alcohol freezes at a lower temperature than water). Polish Pure Spirit is an immense 80 per cent alcohol by volume (abv), and Spirytus Rektyfikowany ('Rectified Spirit') tops 95 per cent. Less strong are the more familiar, neutral (unflavoured) vodkas, such as those produced by Smirnoff and those that originated in the city of Lvov, once a Polish city, but now in the Ukraine.

While unflavoured vodkas lend themselves perfectly to mixed drinks – vodka is the main ingredient of the sea breeze (see page 72), the bloody Mary (see page 61) and the screwdriver (see page 60) – flavoured vodkas have also become very popular. During the mid-19th century in Poland and Russia, more than a hundred styles of spiced and fruit vodka were available, including the viper vodka Zmijowka and the famous Zubrowka. Zmijowka, no longer sold commercially, involved mascerating a viper snake in vodka for several weeks – a recipe that makes the pickled grub in the bottom of a bottle of mescal seem very tame!

Zubrowka is vodka flavoured with bison grass – in each bottle is a blade of grass – a wild herb eaten by European bison roaming the Bialoweiza Forest, in eastern Poland. Other popular flavoured vodkas are cherry, lemon (and lime) and pepper (flavoured with red peppers).

There's an old Russian saying that vodka is only ever drunk for a reason, and that if you happen to have a bottle, you'll find a reason. If you still have trouble justifying drinking vodka, then try these recipes! Really chill your vodka before use: because of their high alcohol content, unflavoured vodkas can be placed in the freezer and will chill without freezing.

kangaroo & vodkatini

method: mixing glass   **glass:** cocktail   **ice:** cubes   **garnish:** lemon twist or olive

These two cocktails are variations on the martini theme. Both use the same ingredients and are stirred, not shaken. The only difference between a kangaroo and a vodkatini is the garnish. Both are shown in the picture.

ingredients

3 to 4 ice cubes

³/₄ measure dry vermouth

1¹/₂ measures vodka

thin strip of lemon peel or 1 olive, to garnish

method

Place the ice cubes in a mixing glass and pour in the dry vermouth and vodka. Stir and strain into a chilled cocktail glass. For a kangaroo, squeeze a thin strip of lemon peel over the glass to release the oil, then drop it into the glass. Or spear an olive on a cocktail stick and add to the glass for a vodkatini.

rose of warsaw

method: mixing glass   **glass:** cocktail   **ice:** cubes

In spite of its name, this Polish-sounding recipe comes from Paris. It's a great excuse for using a really fine Polish vodka, such as Wyborowa, along with a suitably Slavic cherry liqueur, such as Wisniak.

3 to 4 ice cubes

1½ measures Polish vodka

1 measure cherry liqueur (such as Wisniak, Cherry Heering, Luxardo or maraschino)

½ measure Cointreau

dash of angostura bitters

Place the ice in a mixing glass and pour in the remaining ingredients. Stir before straining into a chilled cocktail glass.

screwdriver

method: build   **glass:** highball   **ice:** cubes   **garnish:** orange slice & maraschino cherry

The screwdriver became famous only as recently as the 1950s, and bar legend has it that the drink got its name from an American oilman working in Iraq, who apparently stirred his drink with his screwdriver. There is, however, another account, given by N E Beveridge in *Cups of Valor*. US marines stationed in Teintsin, north-east China, in 1945, made their own 'screwdriver gin', which was stirred with an 18-inch (46-cm) screwdriver.

ingredients

ice cubes

4½ measures orange juice

2 measures vodka

1 orange slice

1 maraschino cherry

1 screwdriver (optional)

method

Fill a highball glass half-full of ice and pour in the orange juice and vodka. Stir – you can use a screwdriver if you like! – and garnish with an orange slice and a maraschino cherry.

Add ½ measure of blue Curaçao to a screwdriver, and you've got 'green eyes'. If you replace the vodka with white rum, you'll get a rumscrew; use 1 measure of vodka and 1 measure of sloe gin, and you have a 'slow screw'! Equal measures of vodka and Wild Turkey result in a 'wild screw'. Take a screwdriver and add 3 measures of 7-Up, and you've got yourself a 'screw-up'.

bloody mary

While the combination of tomato juice and vodka was well already well known as an apéritif, it was in 1921 that the mix was first named, by Fernand, 'Pete' Petiot, of Harry's Bar in Paris. According to some accounts, the spiced mix was named after Mary Pickford, the famous screen actress of the day. In 1933, Petiot travelled to New York at the invitation of John Astor, of the St Regis Hotel, where he became head barman of the King Cole Grill.

2 measures vodka

5 measures tomato juice

1/2 tsp lemon juice

2 dashes Worcestershire sauce

4 drops Tabasco sauce

1 pinch celery salt

1 pinch black pepper

1 stick celery, to garnish

ice cubes

Place the vodka, tomato juice and seasonings into a shaker with some ice cubes, and shake well. Strain into a goblet or large wine glass – over ice, if you wish – and garnish with a celery stick.

If you add 1 measure of gold tequila, you'll get a 'deadly Mary', but if you use only tequila – and no vodka at all – you've got a 'bloody Maria'!

russian night

A whole host of vodka-based drinks have 'Russia' or 'Russian' in their names, even though the vodka used is not Russian. Sibiriskaya, from Siberia, which is made from wheat, has hints of aniseed and liquorice. In this drink, the hint of aniseed is reinstated into the neutral spirit (which has no aroma or flavour of its own) by the addition of a dash of Pernod.

ingredients

3 to 4 ice cubes

1½ measures vodka

2 tsps blue Curaçao

1 dash Pernod

1 maraschino cherry, to garnish

method

Shake all of the ingredients, apart from the cherry, together in a shaker before straining the mix into a chilled cocktail glass. Garnish with a maraschino cherry on a stick.

sex on the beach

method: shaker   **glass:** rocks   **ice:** cubes

This immensely popular drink uses peach 'schnaps', or a peach liqueur, which, rather confusingly, is called a cordial in the USA. There are a number of ways of serving it: shaken and strained over broken ice, or, with reduced quantities, shaken and served straight up as a shooter.

ingredients

8 to 10 ice cubes

1 measure vodka

1 measure peach schnaps
(peach liqueur)

2 measures cranberry juice

2 measures orange juice

method

Put 3 to 4 ice cubes in a shaker and then pour in the vodka, peach schnaps and juices. Shake and strain into an ice-filled rocks glass.

Omit the cranberry juice, and you'll end up with a 'fuzzy navel'.

operation recoverer

method: shaker **glass:** cocktail (straight up) or rocks **ice:** cubes

Ever since it was first distilled, vodka has been flavoured, and by the 19th century, more than a hundred styles were available in Poland and Russia. Among the most popular flavoured vodkas today are the citrus vodkas, and here's a great opportunity for using lemon vodka. You can serve this straight up or, if you prefer, over broken ice, with lots of fruity garnish. Either way, you'll soon be feeling 100 per cent.

ingredients

3 to 4 ice cubes

1 measure lemon vodka

1 measure peach schnaps (peach liqueur)

2 measures mandarin juice

1 tsp grenadine

method

Shake all of the ingredients in a shaker. Either strain into a cocktail glass and serve straight up or strain into a rocks glass half-filled with broken ice and then garnish with fruit and a short straw.

harvey wallbanger

method: build   **glass:** highball   **ice:** cubes   **garnish: orange** slice

The Harvey Wallbanger is said to have derived its name from a Californian surfer (called Harvey), who, having lost a major surfing contest, consoled himself with his usual screwdriver, but with added Galliano. After several of these, he was reported to have bumped into furniture and to have collided with a wall. And so a legend was born!

3 to 4 ice cubes

5 measures orange juice

2 measures vodka

³/₄ measure Galliano

1 slice orange, to garnish

Put the ice cubes in a highball glass and pour in the orange juice and vodka. Sprinkle the Galliano on top and garnish with an orange slice.

Replace the vodka with gold tequila, and you've got a 'Freddy Fudpucker'.

absolut angel

method: shaker   **glass:** cocktail   **ice:** cubes   **garnish:** grated nutmeg

This heavenly recipe, courtesy of the makers of Absolut vodka, makes use of crème de cacao and apple schnaps. According to Ian Wisniewski, one of the UK's foremost authorities on spirits, Austrian 'schnaps sessions' are often accompanied by a drinking song that includes the line, 'Schnaps was his last word, then the angels took him away'!

ingredients

3 to 4 ice cubes

$^1\!/_2$ measure apple schnaps

1 measure Absolut vodka

$^1\!/_2$ tbsp white crème de cacao

1 measure double cream

grated nutmeg, to garnish

method

Put the ice cubes in a shaker and pour over the apple schnaps and the Absolut vodka. Then add the crème de cacao and the cream and shake vigorously. Strain into a cocktail glass and sprinkle with a little grated nutmeg.

slow, comfortable screw

method: shaker   **glass:** highball or collins   **ice:** cubes & broken   **garnish:** maraschino cherry

This is one of those popular cocktails that everyone has heard of, although few know what's in it! The 'slow' means sloe gin, the 'comfortable' means Southern Comfort and the 'screw' comes from the screwdriver: vodka and orange juice.

3 to 4 ice cubes

I measure vodka

³/₄ measure Southern Comfort

³/₄ measure sloe gin

5 measures orange juice

I good scoop broken ice

I maraschino cherry, to garnish

Put the ice cubes in a shaker and pour over the vodka, Southern Comfort, sloe gin and orange juice. Shake and strain into a tall highball or collins glass half-filled with broken ice. Garnish with a maraschino cherry and sip through a straw.

Fancy a 'slow, comfortable screw against the wall'? Then simply sprinkle ¹/₂ measure of Galliano over the top!

tête d'armée

method: shaker   **glass:** cocktail   **ice:** cubes   **garnish:** maraschino cherry

The French-styled name of this cocktail suggests a drink that has a history in cocktail lore. However, a closer look at the ingredients betrays its contemporary origins: Midori, the bright-green, melon-flavoured liqueur from Japan, is a recent innovation, but one that has found a keen following among cocktail-bibbers. The fun part of this cocktail is arranging the blue Curaçao in a pattern over the top!

ingredients

3 to 4 ice cubes

1 measure vodka

1½ measures Midori

1 measure orange juice

1 measure double cream

1 tsp blue Curaçao

1 maraschino cherry, to garnish

method

Shake all of the ingredients, except for the blue Curaçao and the cherry, in a shaker. Strain into a cocktail glass, add the blue Curaçao – don't stir it in – and garnish with a maraschino cherry.

red square

method: shaker   **glass:** cocktail   **ice:** cubes   **garnish:** maraschino cherry

The word 'red' is a popular epithet for some modern cocktails based on vodka. While the addition of vodka may conjure up images of Moscow's Red Square, the red in this drink is provided by grenadine, made from the sweetened juice of pomegranates. White crème de cacao is the third main ingredient, adding a distinctly chocolaty taste.

6 to 8 ice cubes

³/₄ measure vodka

³/₄ measure white crème de cacao

2 tsps lemon juice

1¹/₂ tsp grenadine

1 maraschino cherry, to garnish

Half-fill a shaker with ice and add all of the remaining ingredients, except for the cherry. Strain into a cocktail glass and perch the maraschino cherry on the rim.

vodka silver fizz

method: shaker   **glass:** highball or collins   **ice:** cubes

Fizzes are a group of drinks that date from the 19th century, and that are served in a tall glass no more than half-filled with ice so that the chilled soda water can really fizz and sparkle. It's the addition of the egg white that earns this fizz its silver status. The egg is effectively 'cooked' by the vodka, and it imparts no taste to the drink. This is a great, long drink for a summer's day. It's fruity and slightly bitter, making it very refreshing.

ingredients

10 to 12 ice cubes

2 measures vodka

1 measure lemon juice

3/4 measure sugar syrup

1 egg white

chilled soda water, as required

method

Half-fill a shaker with ice and add all of the remaining ingredients, except for the soda water. Shake firmly to froth up the egg white. Strain into a tall, highball or collins glass half-filled with ice, and top up with chilled soda water.

blue lagoon

method: build   **glass:** highball or collins   **ice:** cubes   **garnish:** lemon slice

Save for a handful of berries, there are few foods or drinks that are naturally blue in colour. Blue Curaçao is a sweet, orange-flavoured liqueur made by infusing orange peel in a spirit. It tastes exactly the same as white (triple-sec) Curaçao – and its red, green, orange and yellow cousins – but it does create a glorious, tropical colour.

3 to 4 ice cubes

³/₄ measure blue Curaçao

1 tsp lemon juice

1¹/₂ measures vodka

chilled lemonade, as required

1 slice lemon, to garnish

Put the ice cubes in a tall, highball or collins glass, and pour over the blue Curaçao, lemon juice and vodka. Top up with chilled lemonade and stir briefly. Perch a lemon slice on the rim of the glass and serve with a straw.

sea breeze

method: shaker   **glass:** highball   **ice:** broken   **garnish:** lime wedge

This very popular, long, fruity drink has become a modern classic. It's quite a 'dry' drink – that is, it's not too sweet – and has a lovely colour, courtesy of cranberry juice. Cranberries – little red berries – are the only fruits whose ripeness is tested by bouncing them over a 5-inch-high (13-cm-high) barrier: those that bounce over are perfect, while those that fail are sent packing!

ingredients

1 good scoop broken ice

2 measures grapefruit juice

3 measures cranberry juice

1½ measures vodka

1 lime wedge, to garnish

method

Put some broken ice into a shaker and pour over the juices and the vodka. Shake and then pour, unstrained, into a highball glass. Finally, garnish the sea breeze with a lime wedge.

Replace the grapefruit juice with pineapple juice, and you've got a 'bay breeze'.

red russian

here are many 'Russians': black Russians, white Russians and even blushin' Russians. All of them are based on vodka and coffee-flavoured liqueurs like Kahlua. The red Russian was created in 1969 in Iceland, by award-winning cocktail barman G Kristjannson, and was originally served straight up.

1 glassful broken ice

1 measure vodka

$^1/_2$ measure cherry brandy

$^1/_2$ measure apricot brandy

Put 1 glassful of broken ice in a shaker and pour in the vodka and two brandies. Shake and then pour, unstrained, into a rocks glass.

vodka cocktails **73**

black russian

method: shake or build   **glass:** cocktail, old-fashioned or highball   **ice:** cubes

Originally, this drink was served as a short drink, either on the rocks or shaken and strained. During the 1950s, cola was added to make a long drink, and a more popular version. Try it both ways.

ingredients

2 to 3 ice cubes

1½ measures vodka

1 measure Tia Maria

cold cola, as required (long version only)

method

Place all of the ingredients in a shaker. Shake and then strain into a cocktail glass. To build a short version, fill an old-fashioned glass two-thirds full of ice cubes, pour in the vodka, then the Tia Maria and stir. For building the long version, fill a highball glass with ice cubes, pour in the vodka and Tia Maria, then top with cold cola. Serve with straws.

kiss and tell

This cocktail makes terrific use of Galliano, a liqueur with a flowery, spicy, herbal flavour. Its sweetness is balanced in this cool, green confection by the vodka and small amount of dry vermouth. The passion fruit is the 'kiss' in this recipe. One of these is enough to make you quite indiscreet!

I good scoop broken ice

I measure vodka

$1/2$ measure Galliano

$1/4$ measure dry vermouth

I tsp blue Curaçao

2 measures orange juice

I measure passion-fruit juice

I slice orange, to garnish

I cherry, to garnish

Fill a rocks glass three-quarters full of broken ice. Now put this ice into a shaker and pour in the remaining ingredients, except for the orange and cherry garnishes. Shake and then pour, unstrained, back into the rocks glass. Garnish with the orange slice and the cherry.

pork chop on toast

method: shaker **glass:** rocks **ice:** cubes; broken **garnish:** maraschino cherry

This fabulously named cocktail makes use of two vodkas: a Russian vodka and a cherry-flavoured vodka. Once you've tried this, you'll never order an 'ordinary' vodka–tonic again! You can actually make your own flavoured vodka by macerating fruit – or herbs and spices, or, indeed, any combination (try horseradish and ginger) – in a vodka of at least 40 per cent alcohol by volume (abv) and leaving it for a month or so.

ingredients

2 to 3 ice cubes

1 measure Russian vodka

1 measure cherry vodka

1 good scoop broken ice

2 measures chilled tonic water

1 maraschino cherry, to garnish

method

Put the ice cubes in a shaker, pour in the two vodkas and shake. Strain into a rocks glass half-filled with broken ice. Top with the chilled tonic water and then pop in a maraschino cherry on a stick.

slow finnish

method: build   **glass:** rocks   **ice:** broken

Cocktail-bibbers will recognise the 'slow' in the name of this drink as signifying sloe gin, which is made by macerating sloes (the fruits of the blackthorn) in gin and maturing it in wooden barrels. The 'Finnish' here is Finlandia vodka, from Finland, which comes in a distinctive, rippled, glass bottle.

1 good scoop broken ice

1 measure sloe gin

1 measure Finlandia vodka

1 tsp dark rum

2 measures cold cola

Fill a rocks glass three-quarters full of broken ice and pour in the sloe gin, Finlandia vodka and rum. Finally, top with cold cola.

Replace the sloe gin with a ²/₃ measure of Quetsch (plum liqueur), and you've got a 'quick Finnish'!

rum cocktails

Famously drunk by pirates and, until recently, officially part of British Royal Navy rations, rum was the most commonly traded contraband for centuries. No one knows exactly how rum got its name: some say that it comes from an English West Country dialect, others say that it comes from saccharum, the Latin for 'sugar'. The home of rum (or ron or rhum, depending on the drink's ethnicity) is in the Caribbean – Jamaica, Martinique, Puerto Rico, Cuba, the Virgin Islands – and a number of coastal countries in Central and South America. It was Christopher Columbus who introduced sugar to the Caribbean, but almost every European nation vied for control of the West Indies and, while differing climates and soils all played their part in producing quite different drinks, each colonial power had its own procedures for producing rum.

Rum can only be made in two ways: it can be distilled directly from the fermented juice of crushed sugar cane; or the sugar itself can be extracted first, and the rum made from the molasses that remain. A further variation requires the addition of a dunder, the residue from a previous distillation, to make a more potent rum. The difference in the raw materials and the duration of the fermentation process will affect the final flavour of the rum.

There are also differences in distillation methods: pot stills and a continuous-still method are both used. A pot still has a pear-shaped pot, usually of copper, in which the materials to be distilled are heated, and a 'swan's neck', which carries the vapour to the condenser. Each distillation is a separate process, after which the still has to be stopped and recharged. If it continued, it would produce a much purer distillate, which would have less flavour. The continuous still, on the other hand, is very efficient at producing purer distillates and light rums (as well as neutral spirits like vodka and gin).

Traditionally, pot stills are used in the French-speaking countries of the Caribbean to distil cane juice, while in the English-speaking countries, Jamaica produces full-bodied rums from molasses and dunder. Guyana produces its own, unique style of rum known as demerara, a dark, but medium-bodied, rum made with molasses in continuous stills. Barbados rum is soft and smoky, and is made in both types of still. Trinidad makes a fine rum in continuous stills, while the Spanish-speaking countries use continuous stills to produce a light-bodied rum from molasses.

All rum is clear and colourless, but for light rum to remain clear, it is first matured in pale, ash-wood barrels for a year and is then transferred to stainless-steel tanks for ageing. Dark rum is left to mature for five to seven years in dark, wooden casks, where it develops its golden or brown colour and a full-bodied flavour. Light or white rums have a more delicate taste than dark rums, and therefore blend superbly with fruit juices and liqueurs without losing their flavours.

mai tai

In 1944, Victor, 'Trader Vic' Bergeron (1901–91) invented the mai tai (Tahitian for 'the best') using the finest ingredients that he could find: a mix of 17-year-old J Wray & Nephew rum, triple sec, orgeat (a non-alcoholic, almond-flavoured syrup), sugar syrup and lime juice. When the mai tai was introduced to Hawaii in 1953, it was so popular that, within a year, all of the stocks of 17-year-old rum in the world had been exhausted, and the cocktail had to be reinvented using a blend of rums.

I glass crushed ice

I measure white rum

I measure dark rum

²/₃ measure triple sec or Cointreau

¹/₃ measure orgeat (or amaretto)

¹/₃ measure sugar syrup

¹/₄ measure grenadine

juice of I lime

I spent lime shell, to garnish

I mint sprig, to garnish

Place all of the ingredients, apart from the lime-shell and mint garnishes, in a shaker and shake briefly. Pour into a collins glass, add the spent lime shell and garnish with the mint sprig. Serve with a straw and a stirrer.

mojito

The mojito can be described as a Cuban mint julep, with its crushed mint leaves in the bottom of the glass. The mojito was an especially popular drink during the US Prohibition at the Bodeguita del Medico Bar in Havana, Cuba.

ingredients

3 to 4 mint sprigs

1 spent lime shell

1 glass crushed or broken ice

2$\frac{1}{2}$ measures white rum

juice of $\frac{1}{2}$ lime

1 dash angostura bitters

$\frac{2}{3}$ measure sugar syrup

3 to 4 ice cubes

2 measures chilled soda water

method

Put the sprigs of mint in the bottom of a collins glass and gently crush them. Add the spent lime shell and fill the glass with crushed or broken ice. Shake the rum, lime juice, angostura bitters and sugar syrup in a shaker with some ice cubes. Strain into the glass and add the soda water. Top with a little more crushed ice if you like, and then gently muddle the mix together. Add a straw.

piña colada

method: shaker or blender   **glass:** poco   **ice:** crushed   **garnish:** pineapple slice & cherry

One of the undisputed cocktail greats, the piña colada comes from Puerto Rico, although the originator of the drink is disputed: some credit Ramon Marrero Perez, of the Carib Hilton, in 1954, others say that it was the creation of Don Ramon Portas Mingot, of La Barrachina Restaurant Bar, in 1963. It is properly served in a poco glass, but any large, attractive glass will contribute to the pleasure of this drink.

1 scoop crushed ice

3 measures white rum

4 measures crushed pineapple or pineapple juice

2 measures coconut cream

1 tsp sugar syrup (optional)

1 slice pineapple, to garnish

1 cherry, to garnish

Shake, or mix in a blender, all of the ingredients, except for the sugar syrup and garnishes. Check for sweetness, and add a little sugar syrup if needed. Strain into a poco glass and garnish with the fruit.

daiquiri & frozen daiqui

method: shaker or blender　　**glass:** champagne saucer　　**ice:** crushed　　**garnish:** lime slice

The original daiquiri, of rum, lime and sugar, was created in Cuba by the American mining engineer Jennings Cox in 1896, and was named after the nearby town of Daiquiri at the suggestion of a colleague. The frozen daiquiri was the creation of Constante Ribailagua, of La Floridita Bar in Havana, where he worked from 1912 until his death in 1952. This is served with crushed ice and, crucially, the lime is squeezed by hand into the mixture, thereby releasing its flavour and aroma.

ingredients

²/₃ measure lime juice

2 measures white rum

1 tsp caster sugar

1 lime slice, to garnish

1 glassful crushed ice (frozen daiquiri only)

method

To make an original daiquiri, shake and strain the lime juice, rum and sugar into a chilled champagne saucer. Garnish with the lime slice.

For frozen daiquiri (pictured), place 1 glassful of crushed ice in a blender and squeeze in the juice from a lime by hand. Pour in the rum and sugar and blend briefly. Pour into a chilled champagne saucer; garnish with a lime slice.

Variations: add ¹/₄ measure of grenadine for a pink daiquiri, or add ¹/₄ measure of crème de cassis for a French daiquiri, the creation of Ernest Luthi, of the Stork Club in York, England, in around 1935.

scorpion

method: blender   **glass:** highball   **ice:** crushed   **garnish:** thin orange slices

This is one of the new generation of long, rum-based drinks that have become modern classics. It is fruity, refreshing and deceptively strong. Substitute Barbadian rum for the light rum for an extra sting in the tail!

2 measures light rum

1 measure brandy

$^1/_2$ measure orgeat (or amaretto, but then you will be adding to the alcohol content)

2 measures orange juice

1$^1/_2$ measures lemon juice

2 good scoops crushed ice

2 to 3 orange slices, to garnish

Blend all of the ingredients, except for the crushed ice and orange slices, in a blender. Pour into a highball glass two-thirds filled with the crushed ice and garnish with the orange slices. Serve with a straw.

chocolate coco

method: shaker   **glass:** large brandy snifter   **ice:** cubes

This drink contains some of the finest ingredients in the Caribbean: rum, coconut, pineapple and chocolate. The rum used here is white and light-bodied, a speciality of the Spanish-speaking countries, and the subtle, coconut flavour comes from Malibu, a white, rum-based, coconut liqueur. Such a luxurious mix requres a really good, dark chocolate, but try not to eat it all first!

ingredients

1 lemon wedge

grated coconut

2 measures pineapple juice

³/₄ measure lemon juice

ice cubes

1 measure Malibu

1 measure light rum

³/₄ measure (about ³/₄oz/20g) melted dark chocolate

method

Run a wedge of lemon around the rim of a large brandy snifter and then dip the rim into some grated coconut. Put the ice cubes in a shaker and pour in the juices, the Malibu and the light rum. Pour in the melted chocolate and shake well. Finally, strain the cocktail into the coconut-rimmed snifter.

cold comfort coffee

method: shaker **glass:** goblet **ice:** crushed & cubes

The 'comfort' in 'cold comfort coffee' is, of course, Southern Comfort, one of America's few 'native' liqueurs, and possibly the oldest. It is made in St Louis, Missouri, from a secret blend of bourbon whisky, peaches, oranges and herbs. The combination of iced coffee, a hint of chocolate (from the crème de cacao) and Southern Comfort make this a great summer 'after-dinner' cooler.

1 good scoop crushed ice

3 to 4 ice cubes

³/₄ measure dark rum

³/₄ measure Southern Comfort

¹/₄ measure dark crème de cacao

4 measures cold, black coffee (sweetened to taste)

Fill a goblet with crushed ice. Place the remaining ingredients in the shaker and shake well. Strain into the goblet.

island breeze

method: build   **glass:** highball   **ice:** cubes

There are plenty of light, cooling breezes blowing through cocktail bars: there's a 'sea breeze' (see page 72), a 'bay breeze' and this gorgeous, yet very simple, rum-and-fruit mix, the 'island breeze'. The island is surely Manhattan, as the drink is the creation of Dale deGroff, of the world-famous Rainbow Room at the top of New York's Rockefeller Plaza.

ingredients

6 to 8 ice cubes

2 dashes angostura bitters

4 measures pineapple juice

1 measure cranberry juice

1 1/2 measures white rum

method

Fill a highball glass with ice and pour in the bitters and juices. Add the rum and stir briefly.

blue hawaiian

method: blender   **glass:** goblet   **ice:** crushed   **garnish:** pineapple slice & maraschino cherry

Rum, pineapple and coconut feature in a mix that's as cool and blue as the Pacific Ocean. The dark, Jamaican-style rum adds extra fullness. This gorgeous cocktail is the creation of Paulo Loureiro, of Claridge's Bar in London's exclusive district of Mayfair.

I glass crushed ice

1 ½ measures white rum

½ measure dark rum

½ measure blue Curaçao

3 measures pineapple juice

I measure coconut cream

I slice pineapple, to garnish

I maraschino cherry, to garnish

Place a glassful of crushed ice in a blender and add all of the remaining ingredients, apart from the pineapple and cherry garnishes. Blend briefly and pour into a goblet. Garnish with the fruit and pop in a short straw.

columbus cocktail

method: shaker   **glass:** large cocktail   **ice:** crushed   **garnish:** lime slice

Christopher Columbus took sugar-cane plants with him on his voyage of discovery to the New World, and found that the climate in the Caribbean was perfect for their cultivation. Later, it was discovered that sugar-cane juice left to ferment in the hot sun made an alcoholic drink that could be distilled into something much stronger: rum.

ingredients

1 glassful crushed ice

1 1/2 measures golden rum

3/4 measure apricot brandy

1 measure lime juice

1 lime slice, to garnish

method

Put a glassful of crushed ice into a shaker and pour in the rum, apricot brandy and lime juice. Shake briefly and pour, unstrained, into a large cocktail glass. Garnish with a lime slice.

brass monkey

method: build   **glass:** highball   **ice:** cubes   **garnish:** orange slice

Rum is synonymous with sailing and the navy: until recently, rum formed part of the official rations of sailors in the British Royal Navy. The brass monkey after which this drink was named was a brass rack on which cannon balls were stored. In very cold weather, the brass monkey would contract and the cannon balls would pop out, hence the expression 'Cold enough to freeze the balls off a brass monkey'!

6 to 8 ice cubes

4 measures orange juice

1 measure vodka

1 measure light rum

1 orange slice, to garnish

Fill a highball glass with ice cubes and pour in the orange juice, vodka and rum. Stir and garnish with a slice of orange and a straw.

mulata

method: shaker   **glass:** champagne saucer   **ice:** crushed

Mulata is the Spanish word for a young female mule, but in parts of the Caribbean, it is also used to describe a girl of mixed European and Afro–Caribbean ancestry. This gorgeous, golden-brown cocktail was devised during the 1940s by Cuban barman José Maria Vazquez, in honour, no doubt, of the island's very many beauties.

ingredients

1³/₄ measures golden rum

¹/₄ measure dark crème de cacao

juice of ¹/₂ lime

1 glassful crushed ice

method

Shake the ingredients briefly with 1 glassful of crushed ice . Pour, unstrained, into a champagne saucer.

venus rum

method: shaker   **glass:** rocks   **ice:** cubes & broken   **garnish:** slice of fruit in season

Venus was the Roman goddess of gardens and spring, as well as of love, so it's appropriate that this cocktail should include both apricot and orange flavours. Apricots get their name from the Latin *praecoquum*, which means 'early ripe' – they are one of the first fruits to appear in spring – while to symbolise his love, Jupiter gave Juno an orange on their wedding day.

2 to 3 ice cubes

1 1/2 measures white rum

1 measure apricot brandy

1/2 measure triple sec or Cointreau

1/2 measure lime juice

1 good scoop broken ice

1 measure chilled soda water

seasonal-fruit slice, to garnish

Put a few ice cubes in a shaker and pour in the rum, apricot brandy, triple sec or Cointreau and lime juice. Shake, and then strain into a rocks glass filled with broken ice. Add the soda water, garnish with a fruit slice and serve with a short straw.

yum-yum

When Christopher Columbus discovered Cuba in 1492, he found an island and climate perfect for the sugar-cane plants that he'd thoughtfully brought with him. Before long, the Spanish realised that cane juice left in the hot sun fermented, and so rum was born. The name of this cocktail really says it all: a delicious mix of rum, coconut and tropical fruit over crushed ice.

ingredients

3 to 4 ice cubes

1 1/2 measures white rum

1/2 measure Malibu (coconut rum)

1 measure mango juice

1 measure peach juice

1/3 measure lime juice

1 good scoop crushed ice

1 lime slice, to garnish

method

Drop the ice cubes into a shaker and add all of the liquids. Shake before straining into a large cocktail glass filled with crushed ice. Garnish with a slice of lime.

platinum blonde

method: shaker **glass:** brandy snifter **ice:** cubes

The original platinum blonde was Hollywood actress Jean Harlow, whose glamorous looks and locks inspired many rivals, but few equals. This mix of golden rum, Grand Marnier (a French, Cognac-based Curaçao) and cream is an elegant tribute to a screen goddess.

3 to 4 ice cubes

1 measure golden rum

1 measure Grand Marnier

3/4 measure double cream

Place all of the ingredients in a shaker, give them a good shake and strain into a brandy snifter.

olaffson's punch

method: shaker   **glass:** goblet   **ice:** crushed   **garnish:** orange & lime twists

Soon after Columbus introduced sugar cane to the Caribbean, every European country involved itself in the West Indies. The Dutch took rum to the East Indies and Australia (where it became the country's first national drink), while the Danes took it back to Scandinavia and Germany. This Scandinavian-sounding cocktail in fact hails from Haiti, famous for its dark, full-bodied rum.

ingredients

1 tsp caster sugar

3 measures orange juice

1 1/2 measures lime juice

1 scoop crushed ice

1 tsp maraschino

2 measures dark rum, preferably Haitian

thin strip each of orange and lime peel, to garnish

method

Dissolve the caster sugar in the orange juice and lime juice. Put some crushed ice into a shaker and pour in the juices, the maraschino and the rum. Shake briefly and pour, unstrained, into a goblet. Twist each strip of peel over the drink to release a drop of oil and then add the twists to the glass. As a final flourish, serve with a short straw.

fluffy duck

method: build   **glass:** highball   **garnish:** strawberry & mint sprig

This drink makes use of advocaat, the Dutch egg-and-brandy liqueur that, legend says, is a version of a thick, avocado drink encountered by Dutch sailors in the East Indies. The most popular advocaat-based drink is the famous snowball, which is made with advocaat, lime cordial and lemonade. Despite its name, the fluffy duck has a real kick!

I measure light rum

I measure advocaat

chilled lemonade, as required

¹/₂ measure single cream

I strawberry, to garnish

I sprig mint, to garnish

Put the rum and the advocaat into a highball glass and almost fill to the top with the chilled lemonade. Trickle the single cream over the back of a spoon on to the surface of the drink and garnish with the strawberry and a sprig of mint.

maragato special

method: shaker   **glass:** large cocktail glass   **ice:** crushed   **garnish:** orange & lime slices

This drink was the creation of Emilio Maragato Gonzalez, of the Florida Hotel Bar in Cuba. Invented in 1920, the recipe was a closely guarded family secret until Emilio's death in 1935.

ingredients

2 to 3 scoops crushed ice

1 measure white rum

3/4 measure dry vermouth

3/4 measure red vermouth

1/2 tsp maraschino

juice of 1/3 orange

juice of 1/2 lime

slices of orange and lime, to garnish

method

Fill a large cocktail glass with crushed ice. Put the remaining ice in a shaker and add all of the ingredients except for the fruit garnish. Shake briefly and strain into the glass and garnish with the fruit slices.

whisky & whiskey cocktails

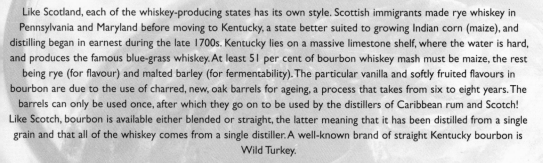

Whisky (spelled without an 'e') in Scotland and Canada, whiskey (spelled with an 'e') in Ireland, the United States and Japan – the name is an abbreviation of *usquebaugh*, the Gaelic word meaning 'water of life'.

Scotch is whisky made only in Scotland. A single-malt whisky will have the character and flavours unique to its location imparted to it by the water, the peat and the flavour of the germinated barley, which is dried over smoky peat fires, mashed, fermented, distilled and matured in wooden caskets for ten to twelve years. A blended Scotch contains anything from a dozen to forty different malts and two or three grain whiskies. In Ireland, the barley is dried in a kiln rather than over a peat fire, which brings forth a different flavour.

Like Scotland, each of the whiskey-producing states has its own style. Scottish immigrants made rye whiskey in Pennsylvania and Maryland before moving to Kentucky, a state better suited to growing Indian corn (maize), and distilling began in earnest during the late 1700s. Kentucky lies on a massive limestone shelf, where the water is hard, and produces the famous blue-grass whiskey. At least 51 per cent of bourbon whiskey mash must be maize, the rest being rye (for flavour) and malted barley (for fermentability). The particular vanilla and softly fruited flavours in bourbon are due to the use of charred, new, oak barrels for ageing, a process that takes from six to eight years. The barrels can only be used once, after which they go on to be used by the distillers of Caribbean rum and Scotch! Like Scotch, bourbon is available either blended or straight, the latter meaning that it has been distilled from a single grain and that all of the whiskey comes from a single distiller. A well-known brand of straight Kentucky bourbon is Wild Turkey.

Rye, historically the first whiskey of the United States, has a spicy, even minty, flavour because of the use of a minimum of 51 per cent rye grains (the rest being maize and barley). It is matured for about four years in new, charred, oak barrels.

Tennessee whiskey must, by law, be produced in the state of that name. It is filtered through wood charcoal and is therefore very mild. Some of the best-known brands – like Jack Daniels, from Lynchburg, which is filtered through maple chippings – have a distinct flavour from bourbon because they are produced from a sour mash that contains previously fermented yeast. Fresh yeast makes a sweet mash, while, in Tennessee, the already fermented yeast (similar to that used to make sourdough bread) makes for a sour mash.

quebec

method: mixing glass   **glass:** cocktail   **ice:** cubes

Only in Britain and Canada is whisky spelled without an 'e'. Canadian whisky is smooth and light-bodied, which makes it perfect for cocktails. This cocktail also uses Noilly Prat, a French dry vermouth made in Marseilles. This is a perfect combination for bilingual Quebec: indeed, Noilly's famous slogan said, 'Say Noilly Prat, and your French is perfect'.

ingredients

3 to 4 ice cubes

1 ½ measures Canadian whisky

2 tsps Noilly Prat dry vermouth

1 tsp Amer Picon

1 tsp maraschino

method

Stir the ingredients together in a mixing glass and then strain into a cocktail glass.

canada cocktail

method: build   **glass:** rocks   **ice:** broken   **garnish:** mint sprig

With such a name, this cocktail demands Canadian whisky. The most famous name in Canadian distilling is Seagram's. Once a relatively small whisky firm in Ontario, Seagram's was bought by Sam Bronfman in 1926, and by the mid-1950s, it was the world's largest distiller and occupied the Seagram Building in New York, a landmark in modern architecture designed by Ludwig Mies van der Rohe.

1 scoop broken ice

3 drops angostura bitters

½ measure Cointreau

1½ measures Canadian whisky

1 mint sprig, to garnish

Put some broken ice into a rocks glass and add the angostura bitters, the Cointreau and the Canadian whisky. Garnish with a sprig of mint.

tuna on rye

method: build   **glass:** rocks   **ice:** broken

Some cocktail aficionados maintain that some of the strange names of drinks were speakeasy code names used to confuse police infiltrators. Others say that they grew out of American 'diner-speak', in which the most mundane dishes, like poached eggs on toast, are called something far more exotic, in this case, 'Adam and Eve on a raft'. In this drink, the rye is rye whiskey, but the tuna – who knows?

ingredients

1 scoop broken ice

1 measure red vermouth

1 ½ measures rye whiskey

2 measures ginger ale

method

Half-fill a rocks glass with broken ice and pour in the vermouth and rye. Finally, add the ginger ale.

pink elephant

Pink elephants were what those who were somewhat worse for wear reported seeing after a hard night's drinking! This lemon–whiskey-flavoured cocktail uses bourbon, a whiskey distilled from a fermented mash of at least 51 per cent corn and aged for between six and eight years in charred, new, oak casks which, by US law, can only be used once.

1 scoop crushed ice

3 to 4 ice cubes

2 measures bourbon

$^3/_4$ measure lemon juice

$^1/_3$ measure grenadine

1 tsp egg white

1 lemon slice, to garnish

1 cherry, to garnish

Fill a cocktail glass with crushed ice. Drop the ice cubes into a shaker and add all of remaining ingredients, except for the fruit garnishes. Shake well and strain into the cocktail glass. Garnish with a lemon slice and a cherry.

plank-walker

method: build   **glass:** rocks   **ice:** broken

'Walking the plank' was a method of execution reputedly favoured by pirates: the plank extended over the side of the ship and the unfortunate victim landed in the sea. No such fate awaits the bibber of this cocktail. On the contrary, the reputedly life-enhancing benefits of the 130 herbs and spices in the Chartreuse should ensure that you live another day!

ingredients

1 scoop broken ice

1½ measures Scotch whisky

½ measure red vermouth

½ measure yellow Chartreuse

method

Fill a rocks glass three-quarters full of broken ice and pour in the remaining ingredients.

morning-glory fizz

method: shaker   **glass:** collins   **ice:** cubes   **garnish:** orange slice

Fizzes were first mentioned during the 1870s. This is similar to a Collins (see page 35), but is always shaken before the soda (or another sparkling mixer) is added. Fizzes are traditionally served in the morning, or at midday at the latest.

1 tsp caster sugar

1¹/₃ measures lemon juice

6 to 8 ice cubes

1 dash angostura bitters

2 measures Scotch whisky

¹/₄ measure egg white

4 measures soda water

1 slice orange, to garnish

Dissolve the caster sugar in the lemon juice. Put half of the ice cubes in a shaker and pour in the juice, bitters, Scotch and egg white. Shake well and strain into a collins glass half-filled with the remaining ice. Top with soda water and garnish with a slice of orange. Serve with a muddler.

kentucky kernel

Like all good cocktail names, Kentucky kernel is a pun: 'Kentucky' refers to Kentucky bourbon, while 'kernel' refers to the stone of the apricot in the apricot brandy.

ingredients

1 scoop broken ice

1½ measures bourbon

½ measure apricot brandy

1 measure grapefruit juice

1 tsp grenadine

method

Place the broken ice in a shaker and add the remaining ingredients. Shake, then pour, unstrained, into a rocks glass.

mississippi magic

method: blender   **glass:** goblet   **ice:** crushed

This cocktail contains both bourbon and Southern Comfort. The originator of the liqueur's secret recipe is reputed to have been one M W Heron, who was working in New Orleans during the 1880s, but who launched his liqueur in his bar on Beale Street, in Memphis, before moving to St Louis, Missouri. In case you hadn't noticed, all three great cities are on the mighty Mississippi river.

$1/2$ peach

1 glassful crushed ice

1 measure bourbon

1 measure Southern Comfort

$1/2$ measure dry vermouth

1 measure mandarin juice

1 measure pineapple juice

$1/4$ measure lime juice

Purée the peach half. Put 1 glassful of crushed ice into a blender and pour in the remaining ingredients, including the puréed peach. Blend briefly, and pour, unstrained, into a goblet. Serve with a straw.

wild cherry

method: build   **glass:** highball   **ice:** cubes   **garnish:** cherry & mint sprig

The 'wild' in this cocktail's name refers to Wild Turkey, a famous brand of Kentucky straight-bourbon whiskey. There are two strengths available – 43 per cent abv (US 86 per cent proof) and a mighty 50.5 per cent abv (US 101 per cent proof) – as well as a Wild Turkey liqueur. The 'cherry' refers to the cherry brandy, of course.

ingredients

3 to 4 ice cubes

½ measure cherry brandy

¼ measure white crème de cacao

1½ measures Wild Turkey bourbon

4 measures chilled cherryade

1 cherry, to garnish

1 mint sprig, to garnish

method

Put the ice cubes into a highball glass and pour in the cherry brandy, white crème de cacao and Wild Turkey bourbon. Top with the chilled cherryade and, finally, garnish with a cherry and a mint sprig.

irish blackthorn

method: mixing glass **glass:** rocks **ice:** cubes

The blackthorn – whose fruits are the sloes used to make sloe gin – provides the wood traditionally used to make shillelaghs (clubs or cudgels). By rights, this cocktail should use Irish whiskey. The difference between this and Scotch is that in Ireland, the barley is dried in a kiln rather than over a peat fire.

6 to 8 ice cubes

1½ measures Irish whiskey

1½ measures dry vermouth

3 dashes Pernod

3 dashes angostura bitters

Put half of the ice cubes in a mixing glass and pour in the remaining ingredients. Strain into a rocks glass with the rest of the ice.

three rivers

method: shaker   **glass:** rocks   **ice:** broken & cubes

Invented in Canada, where it is well known by its French name, trois rivières, this drink is now enjoyed around the world. Canadian whisky is the preferred choice, here mixed with the patented French apéritif Dubonnet and the clear Curaçao triple sec.

ingredients

1 scoop broken ice

3 to 4 ice cubes

2 measures Canadian whisky

1 measure Dubonnet

1 measure triple sec (or Cointreau)

method

Half-fill a rocks glass with broken ice. Place the remaining ingredients in a shaker and shake. Strain into the glass.

the waldorf cocktail

method: mixing glass   **glass:** cocktail   **ice:** crushed

A classic cocktail created in honour of one of the finest hotels in New York, and one of the city's great architectural masterpieces. Traditionally, bourbon is the whiskey of choice, but by trying different blends, you can subtly alter the end result.

1 good scoop crushed ice

1 dash angostura bitters

1 measure sweet vermouth

1 measure Pernod

2 measures bourbon

Put a good scoop of crushed ice in a mixing glass and add the angostura bitters, sweet vermouth, Pernod and bourbon. Stir well and strain into a chilled cocktail glass.

lark

method: build   **glass:** goblet   **ice:** cubes   **garnish:** orange & lemon slices, cherry

A lark is both a bird and a word used to describe good-natured mischief – a perfect description for this fruity mix. Scotch (whisky made only in Scotland can be called this) is the whisky of choice, and is deserving of Grand Marnier, the Cognac-based, orange liqueur of the highest quality.

ingredients

3 to 4 ice cubes

1 measure Scotch whisky

1 measure Grand Marnier

$1/4$ measure grenadine

$1/4$ measure lemon juice

4 measures chilled orangeade

2 to 3 orange and lemon slices, to garnish

1 cherry, to garnish

method

Put the ice cubes into a goblet and, with the exception of the orange and lemon slices and cherry, pour the remaining ingredients into the glass, topping with the chilled orangeade. Garnish with the fruit and add a straw.

sky highball

method: build   **glass:** highball   **ice:** cubes   **garnish:** lemon twist

The highball was invented by New York barman Patrick Duffy (no relation to the star of the television show 'Dallas') in 1895. Duffy used one spirit, soda or ginger ale and a twist of lemon. By the 1930s, triple sec and grenadine had made their way into the recipe, and by the 1950s, fruit juices had been added. Today's highballs use two mixers – one sparkling – but still only one base spirit. The blue Curaçao provides the 'sky' in this recipe.

6 to 8 ice cubes

5 measures pineapple juice

2 measures Scotch whisky

1 tsp blue Curaçao

thin strip of lemon peel, to garnish

Fill a highball glass three-quarters full of ice. Pour in the pineapple juice and the Scotch and sprinkle the blue Curaçao on top. Twist the lemon peel over the drink to release its oil, and then drop it into the glass.

whisky & whiskey cocktails **111**

fancy free

method: shaker **glass:** cocktail **ice:** cubes

Fancy Free was the name of a 1944, one-act ballet by Jerome Robbins. Set to music by Leonard Bernstein, it told the story of three sailors on shore leave in New York. It was a real hit, and became the point of departure for the great movie musical *On the Town*. Appropriately, this cocktail uses rye whiskey, the first whiskey to be made in the USA, and which dates back to the late 1600s.

ingredients

1 lemon wedge, for rimming

caster sugar, for rimming

3 to 4 ice cubes

1½ measures rye whiskey

2 dashes maraschino

1 dash orange bitters

1 dash angostura bitters

method

Rub the rim of a cocktail glass with a wedge of lemon and then dip it into the caster sugar. Place some ice cubes in a shaker and pour in the remaining ingredients. Shake and then strain into the sugar-rimmed cocktail glass.

rattlesnake

method: shaker   **glass:** rocks   **ice:** crushed

Hollywood actor, and king of the one-liners, W C Fields said, 'I always carry a little whiskey with me in case I see a snake. I always carry a snake as well.' As well as this cocktail of whisky and Pernod, an aniseed-flavoured *pastis*, there is a pousse-café rattlesnake constructed of layers of Irish Cream liqueur, coffee liqueur and white crème de cacao. Both versions would, no doubt, have met with Field's approval.

1 good scoop crushed ice

2 measures of your favourite whisky

1 tsp lemon juice

1 tsp sugar syrup

½ the white of 1 egg

several dashes of Pernod

Place the ice in a cocktail shaker and pour in the remaining ingredients. Shake vigorously to froth up the egg white, then strain into a chilled rocks glass.

dundee dream

method: shaker   **glass:** highball   **ice:** broken   **garnish:** cherry & orange slice

Dundee lies on the Firth of Tay, in eastern Scotland, and is famous among many other things – for its rich fruit cake. This fruity cockta naturally uses Scotch whisky, along with sweet sherry, mandarin juic and lime juice. Dry ginger ale turns it into a very refreshing, long drink.

ingredients

1 scoop broken ice

1½ measures Scotch whisky

½ measure sweet sherry

1 measure mandarin juice

½ measure lime juice

3 measures dry ginger ale

1 cherry, to garnish

1 slice orange, to garnish

method

Place the broken ice in a shaker and pour in the Scotch, sherry and the two juices. Shake and then pour, unstrained, into a highball glass. Top with the ginger ale and garnish with a cherry and slice of orange.

rare beef

method: build　　**glass:** rocks　　**ice:** broken　　**garnish:** cherry

This is a cocktail whose name refers to its ingredients: the 'rare' indicates that the whisky involved is J & B, on whose label the word appears, and which, in Scotland, means 'exceptional' or 'choice'. The 'beef' refers to the gin: Beefeater, a brand of London dry gin on whose label is depicted a yeoman of the Royal Guard of the Tower of London, otherwise known as a 'Beefeater'.

I scoop broken ice

I measure red vermouth

$^1/_2$ measure J & B whisky

I measure Beefeater gin

I measure lemonade

I cherry, to garnish

Half-fill a rocks glass with broken ice. Pour in the vermouth, the whisky and the gin and top with lemonade. Add a cherry on a stick.

For a Southern rare beef, replace half of the red vermouth with Southern Comfort.

brandy cocktails

In the 18th century, Samuel Johnson wrote, 'Claret is the liquor for boys, port for men; but he who aspires to be a hero must drink brandy'. If only Johnson were alive today to see how many women enjoy brandy, too!

Brandy, a warming, sensual spirit distilled from wine, is produced in many countries, and consequently takes several forms. Some say that brandy was first discovered in the middle of the 13th century in France, during attempts to make a medicinal drink; others, that an alchemist in the 15th century buried his barrel of precious *aqua vitae* in his garden to keep it out of the hands of looting soldiers. The poor fellow was killed, and his barrel was not discovered until years later. Half of the liquor had evaporated, but what remained was rich and smooth.

Generally, after two distillations, the clear, colourless brandy is given its nut-brown colour and flavour by ageing it in oak barrels. The longer it ages, the more refined its flavour. The king of brandies is Cognac, which hails from a specific area centred on the town of Cognac, in the Charentes region of France. To be a true Cognac, French law dictates that the brandy may only be made from specified white grapes grown and distilled in a given area. Twice distilled and aged in oak barrels for at least two years, the end result is 80 per cent alcohol by volume (abv). Three stars, or 'VS', mean that the Cognac has matured for two years in the barrel; 'VSOP', 'Vieux', 'VO' and 'reserve' mean that the Cognac has aged in the barrel for at least four years; 'VVSOP' and 'Grand Reserve' are Cognacs that have matured for at least five years; 'Extra', 'Napoleon', 'XO', Très Vieux' and 'Vieille reserve' are aged for between six and ten years in their barrels.

Armagnac is a pale-golden-coloured French brandy with a dry, fiery taste. Only white grapes from the Haute-Armagnac, Tenareze and Bas-Armagnac regions of Gascony are allowed under French law. The distillation takes place after the grape harvest (from October to April), and, unlike Cognac, Armagnac has only one distillation (although recently French law has been relaxed to allow double distillation, which speeds up the ageing process that occurs in oak barrels). Three stars on the label mean that it has been matured for at least two years; 'VSOP', for at least five years; 'Napoleon' and 'XO', for at least six years; and 'Hors d'Age' means that it has aged for at least ten years in the barrel. A vintage year on the label indicates the year of harvest: gorgeous it tastes, too, and really far too good to mix with anything, except friends!

Outside France, brandy is produced wherever grapes are grown, in both the Old World of Spain, Portugal, Italy, Greece and Germany, and the New World, particularly in California, in the United States, and in Chile, in South America.

b and b

One 'B' in this cocktail's name is for Benedictine; the other is for brandy (preferably Cognac) deserving of such a fine companion. Benedictine was first formulated in 1510, by Benedictine monks at their abbey at Fécamp, in Normandy, France. The production process involves some 27 herbs, plants, fruit peels and flowers, takes three years and is completed only after a further four years of ageing.

3 to 4 ice cubes

1 measure brandy or Cognac

1 measure Benedictine

Place all of the ingredients in a mixing glass and stir. Strain into a liqueur or cordial glass.

b and b collins

method: mixing glass   **glass:** collins or highball   **ice:** crushed   **garnish:** lemon slice

The Collins probably got its name from one John Collins – a famous head waiter at Limmers, a London coffee house and hotel situated in Conduit Street from 1790 to 1817 – who reputedly made the first Collins using gin. This version is made with brandy, with Benedictine sprinkled over the top.

ingredients

2 good scoops crushed ice

2 measures brandy or Cognac

juice of ½ lemon

1 tsp sugar syrup

chilled soda water, as required

1 measure Benedictine

1 lemon slice, to garnish

method

Place 2 good scoops of crushed ice into a mixing glass and pour in the brandy, lemon juice and sugar syrup. Stir well, strain into a chilled collins or highball glass and top with chilled soda water. Carefully float the Benedictine on the surface and garnish with a slice of lemon.

brandy alexander

method: shaker   glass: cocktail or champagne saucer   ice: cubes   garnish: grated chocolate or nutmeg

Originally, the Alexander was a gin-based drink, but the use of brandy has made it into one of the most sophisticated after-dinner cocktails, in spite of its very simple construction. There is also a whole range of Alexanders that has since been developed, like the coffee Alexander and Alexander's sister, a treat for mint-lovers (see page 31).

2 to 3 ice cubes

1⅓ measures dark crème de cacao

1⅓ measures double cream

1⅓ measures brandy

grated chocolate or nutmeg, to garnish

Put 2 or 3 ice cubes in a shaker and add the crème de cacao and the cream. Add the brandy and shake well. Strain into a cocktail glass or champagne saucer and decorate with grated chocolate or nutmeg.

brandy flip

method: shaker **glass:** champagne saucer **ice:** cracked **garnish:** grated nutmeg

Flips take their name from the old practice of flipping the drinks over and over between two vessels or glasses in order to make them smooth; today, they are made in a shaker. Dating from the 17th century, flips typically then contained beaten eggs, sugar, spices, rum and some hot ale, all mulled with an iron loggerhead or poker heated in the fire. Today, flips are served cold, short and with nutmeg sprinkled over the top.

ingredients

1 scoop cracked ice

2 measures brandy

1/2 measure sugar syrup

1 small egg, beaten

grated nutmeg, to garnish

method

Place all of the ingredients, apart from the grated nutmeg, in a shaker and shake vigorously to froth up the egg. Strain and pour into a champagne saucer. Sprinkle with nutmeg.

Make a flip using Scotch whisky, bourbon, tequila, sherry, vodka, or dark rum by replacing the brandy with your pet tipple.

sidecar

This sharp-tasting cocktail makes a terrific apéritif. Legend has it that the sidecar was invented by, and was consequently named after, a somewhat eccentric, military man, who used to arrive at Harry's New York Bar, in Paris, France, in the sidecar of his chauffeur-driven motorcycle.

2 to 3 ice cubes

1½ measures brandy or Cognac

1 measure Cointreau

1 measure lemon juice (or more to taste)

Place 2 or 3 ice cubes in a shaker and pour in the brandy, Cointreau and lemon juice. Shake and then strain into a cocktail glass.

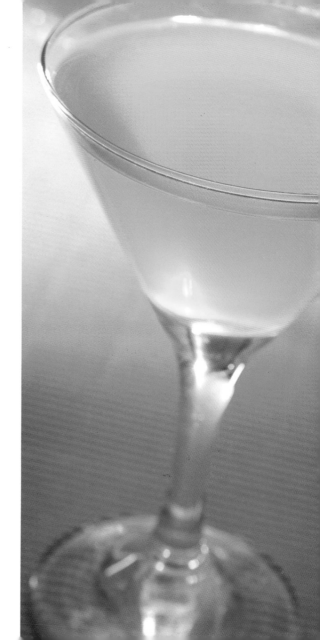

stinger

The stinger, like many famous cocktails, has its origins in America's Prohibition era, and is a true classic. Originally, it was served straight up, but it is now popular as a sipping drink on the rocks. It's a very easy cocktail to make, and has a spicy freshness that makes it ideal as an after-dinner drink.

ingredients

3 to 4 ice cubes

1 ½ measures brandy or Cognac

¾ measure white crème de menthe

method

Put 3 or 4 ice cubes into a mixing glass and pour in the brandy and crème de menthe. Stir and then strain into a cocktail glass.

between the sheets

method: shaker   **glass:** cocktail   **ice:** cubes

A classic cocktail from the 1930s, with a slightly risqué name and a tangy, fruity taste to match. This is a perfect drink for the evening: pre-dinner, pre-theatre or, perhaps, even pre-bedtime!

3 to 4 ice cubes

1½ measures Cognac

1 measure light rum

1 measure Cointreau

1 dash lemon juice

Shake all of the ingredients together in a shaker. Strain and pour into a cocktail glass.

french connection

method: build   **glass:** rocks or old-fashioned   **ice:** cubes

This bitter-sweet drink is a simple mix of Cognac and amaretto, an almond-flavoured liqueur made in Italy from apricot kernels. It is reputed to have been first made in Saronno, in 1525, as a tribute to the artist Bernardino Luini from his lover and model.

3 to 4 ice cubes

1 measure Cognac

$^3/_4$ measure amaretto

Half-fill a rocks or old-fashioned glass with ice cubes. Pour over the Cognac and amaretto and stir in the glass.

ritz cocktail

method: shaker   **glass:** champagne flute   **ice:** cubes   **garnish:** ½ orange slice

A cocktail for when you're 'putting on the Ritz'. This aromatic, champagne cocktail makes a splendid apéritif or after-dinner drink. Actually, it's so good that you can drink it any time that the mood takes you!

3 to 4 ice cubes

¾ measure brandy or Cognac

¾ measure Cointreau

¾ measure orange juice

chilled champagne (or sparkling white wine), as required

½ slice orange, to garnish

Into a shaker containing 3 or 4 ice cubes, pour the brandy, Cointreau and orange juice. Shake and strain into a champagne flute. Top with chilled champagne or sparkling white whine and perch the ½ slice of orange on the rim of the glass at a rakish angle.

brandy cocktail

method: mixing glass   **glass:** cocktail   **ice:** cubes   **garnish:** maraschino cherry

There are numerous versions of the brandy cocktail, and all are delicious. Try these variations. Both are made using the same method, and both are served in cocktail glasses. Brandy cocktail 1 is illustrated at left.

ingredients

Brandy cocktail 1

3 to 4 ice cubes

1½ measures brandy

1 tsp sugar

3 dashes angostura bitters

1 maraschino cherry, to garnish

Brandy cocktail 2

3 to 4 ice cubes

2 measures brandy

1 measure dry vermouth

1 measure Grand Marnier

2 dashes angostura bitters

1 thin strip orange peel

method

Brandy cocktail 1
Stir all of the ingredients in a mixing glass, then strain into a cocktail glass and garnish with a cherry.

Brandy cocktail 2
Put some ice cubes into a mixing glass and pour in the brandy, dry vermouth and Grand Marnier. Stir well. Add the bitters to a cocktail glass, swirling them round the sides to coat the glass. Strain the mixture from the mixing glass into the cocktail glass and squeeze the orange peel over the glass to release the oil before discarding it.

rolls royce

method: shaker   **glass:** cocktail   **ice:** crushed

This very elegant cocktail is also very simple to make. It consists of equal measures of orange juice, Cognac and Cointreau, an orange-flavoured liqueur that has been made by the Cointreau family since 1849.

2 to 3 scoops crushed ice

1 measure Cognac

1 measure Cointreau

1 measure orange juice

Place 2 or 3 scoops of crushed ice into a shaker and pour in the Cognac, Cointreau and orange juice. Shake well and then pour into a well-chilled cocktail glass.

charleston

method: mixing glass   **glass:** highball   **ice:** cubes

The charleston was probably the most famous dance to emerge from the Prohibition era, and was named after the city in South Carolina. Fast and furious, the charleston was originally a solo dance, and was popularised during the 1920s by the big musical revues, especially in Harlem, New York. One of the greatest exponents of this speeded-up and syncopated foxtrot was the great Josephine Baker. This cocktail is as appealing today as it was during the Jazz Age.

ingredients

8 to 10 ice cubes

1 measure cherry brandy

1 measure Mandarine Napoleon liqueur

lemonade, as required

method

Fill a highball glass with ice. Put 2 to 3 ice cubes in a mixing glass and pour over the cherry brandy and Mandarine Napoleon. Stir well, then strain into the highball glass. Finally, top with lemonade.

egg nog

The origin of this drink is probably the noggin, a small glass of strong beer to which was often added a beaten egg in order to thicken it. Today, brandy, or rum, is used instead of beer, and the egg nog is now one of the few cocktails that doesn't use ice. It's a wonderfully warming drink, ideal for cold, winter days or, traditionally, Christmas mornings spent in front of a blazing fire.

1 measure brandy

1 measure dark rum

1 fresh egg

1 dash sugar syrup

5 measures full-cream milk

grated nutmeg, to garnish

Pour the brandy, rum, egg and sugar syrup into a shaker and shake vigorously to create a creamy consistency. Strain into a highball glass, add the milk and stir gently. Sprinkle a little grated nutmeg over the top and serve at room temperature.

the international

method: mixing glass   **glass:** cocktail   **ice:** crushed

The name of this cocktail hints at the diverse 'nationalities' of the ingredients. While the main ingredients are French (Cognac and Cointreau), international relations are established with Greece (ouzo) and Russia (vodka).

ingredients

1 scoop crushed ice

2 measures Cognac

$\frac{1}{2}$ measure vodka

$\frac{1}{2}$ measure ouzo

$\frac{1}{2}$ measure Cointreau

method

Put some crushed ice into a mixing glass and add the Cognac, vodka, ouzo and Cointreau. Stir well and strain into a well-chilled cocktail glass. As a final flourish, garnish with the flags of all nations!

cherry blossom

There are a number of versions of this cocktail; one has nothing to do with cherries, and is made with gin. This version uses cherry brandy, as well as Cognac, and a dash or two of grenadine for extra redness. In some bars, the rim of the glass is dipped in cherry brandy and then into sugar – if you have an extra-sweet tooth, then try that as well.

3 to 4 ice cubes

³/₄ measure Cognac

³/₄ measure cherry brandy

³/₄ measure lemon juice

2 tsps Cointreau

2 tsps grenadine

1 maraschino cherry, to garnish (optional)

Shake all of the ingredients, apart from the maraschino cherry, together in a shaker. Strain into a cocktail glass. Pop the maraschino cherry on the rim if you like.

brandy zoom

method: shaker   **glass:** cocktail   **ice:** cubes

Zooms were a 'family' of mixed drinks that were popular during the 1930s, but sadly, had disappeared from bars by the end of that decade. You can make a zoom with any base spirit, including gin, rum and whisky, but somehow brandy works best.

ingredients

3 to 4 ice cubes

1 ½ measures brandy

¾ measure cream

2 tsps honey

method

Shake all of the ingredients together in a shaker. Strain into a cocktail glass and serve.

james

Delicate and dry, this cocktail is a perfect balance of flavours and an ideal, elegant, after-dinner drink. Cognac is here combined with gin, the dryness of which is balanced by the sweetness of the yellow Chartreuse. One of the oldest liqueurs, Chartreuse is still produced by Carthusian monks, and only three monks know the secret formula at any one time.

3 to 4 ice cubes

³/₄ measure Cognac

³/₄ measure gin

³/₄ measure yellow Chartreuse

1 green maraschino cherry, to garnish

Put 3 to 4 ice cubes in a mixing glass and pour over the Cognac, gin and yellow Chartreuse. Mix, and then strain into a cocktail glass and perch the green maraschino cherry on the rim.

picasso

method: shaker   **glass:** cocktail   **ice:** cubes

Many artists and writers are celebrated in cocktails: there's the bellini, the hemingway special, the verdi, the caruso and the marilyn monroe. Mozart even has a chocolate-cream liqueur named after him. This cocktail pays homage to the undoubted master of the Modern movement, Pablo Picasso.

ingredients

3 to 4 ice cubes

1 measure Cognac

³/₄ measure Dubonnet

2 tsps lemon juice

4 dashes sugar syrup

method

Shake all of the ingredients in a shaker and then strain into a cocktail glass.

calvados & applejack cocktails

There is practically no end to the variety of fruit that can be enjoyed in alcoholic form, although some fruits are more suitable than others. It's all a matter of the fruit's sugar content.

One fruit spirit is Calvados, an apple brandy made from the cider produced in Normandy, France. Under strict French laws, the name 'Calvados' can only be applied to the cider distillations that come from just 11 specified areas. After distillation, the liquid is stored in oak or chestnut barrels and matured for at least two years. The older the Calvados, the more amber-brown the colour, and the more velvety and aromatic the taste. Such a fine spirit doesn't usually accompany meals in France: instead, it's served between courses at formal dinner parties as an aid to digestion and for pepping up the appetite, ready to tackle the remaining dishes of the feast! For many Frenchmen (and women), Calvados is the last drink of the day, or, indeed, the first. Café-Calva, a strong coffee with Calvados on the side, or strong coffee fortified with Calvados, is a great way to start the day!

Like that used for Cognac (and Armagnac), Calvados is distinguished by a labelling system to indicate the number of years that it has been aged in the barrel: three stars means two years at least; 'Vieux' and 'Reserve' indicate at least three years; 'VO', 'Vieille Reserve' or 'VSOP' guarantee at least four years' maturation; while 'Extra' or 'XO', 'Napoleon', 'Hors d'Age' and 'Age Inconnu' (literally, 'unknown age') indicate that the Calvados has been quietly waiting for its moment for at least six years.

There are many other apple brandies, which cannot be called Calvados, but are nevertheless fine products. These apple brandies, including French products made outside the controlled regions, are known as eaux-de-vie de pomme ('the water of life of apples'). Applejack is a delightful, American apple brandy, and a speciality of New England, while Spain, too, produces its own version, called *aquardiente di sidre*. Meanwhile, from Austria and Germany comes *Obstler*, made from fermented apples (or pears, or a mixture of the two). The variety of fruit must be listed on the label, and the majority of these brandies boast between 80 and 100 per cent alcohol by volume (abv).

Young Calvados, applejack and apple brandies in general are increasingly popular when drunk on the rocks or in cocktails. Here are a few recipes for you to try. I'm pretty sure that that maxim 'An apple a day keeps the doctor away' can be applied here, too!

boston

Many cocktails are named after cities, but few cities can match the number named after Boston, Massachusetts! While the boston cocktail is a gin- and apricot-brandy-based mix, the boston punch and the boston both make use of the flavour imparted by apples. In this cocktail, the French apple brandy Calvados is used.

ingredients

3 to 4 ice cubes

I measure Calvados

2 tsps gin

2 tsps Scotch whisky

method

Put the ice cubes in a mixing glass and pour in the Calvados, gin and Scotch. Strain into a cocktail glass.

calvados sour

The sour was a drink that came onto the scene during the 1850s, with the whiskey sour. These drinks became very popular, and even had their own, stemmed glass, although today they are generally served in a rocks or old-fashioned glass. During the 1880s, soda water began to be included, but always as an option.

6 to 8 ice cubes

³/₄ measure lemon juice

2 tsps sugar syrup

1½ measures Calvados

½ slice orange, to garnish

1 maraschino cherry, to garnish

chilled, sparkling, mineral water, as required (optional)

Half-fill a rocks glass with ice. Place the remaining ice in a shaker and pour in the lemon juice, sugar syrup and Calvados. Shake well and then strain into the rocks glass. Garnish with the ½ slice of orange and a maraschino cherry. Top with a dash or two of chilled, sparkling, mineral water if you like.

white wing

method: shaker   **glass:** cocktail   **ice:** cubes

One of the specialities of the Normandy region of northern France, the finest Calvados comes only from the *appellation controlée* region known as the Pays d'Auge. This cocktail combines the flavours of apple with mint, and consequently makes the perfect *digestif*.

ingredients

3 to 4 ice cubes

1 measure Calvados

1 measure white crème de menthe

method

Place some ice cubes in a shaker and pour in the Calvados and white crème de menthe. Shake well and strain into a cocktail glass.

138   calvados & applejack cocktails

vermont

method: shaker   **glass:** cocktail   **ice:** cubes

The state of Vermont is known as the 'Lone Pine State', an emblem that features on the state flag, where it is set against a background of the Green Mountains, a range popular for winter sports. This fruity mix of apple brandy and grenadine is ideal for après-ski or following a hearty, New England supper.

3 to 4 ice cubes

1 ½ measures Calvados or applejack

2 tsps grenadine

2 tsps lemon juice

Shake all of the ingredients together in a shaker. Strain into a cocktail glass, take a sip and then feel the colour come back into your cheeks!

applejack rabbit

method: shaker   **glass:** cocktail   **ice:** cubes   **garnish:** ½ slice orange

While France produces Calvados, New England is famous for its own apple brandy, known as applejack. This cocktail also uses maple syrup, the sap collected from sugar, red and silver maple trees in spring – the same time that the long-eared jack rabbits also start to feel their 'sap' rising!

ingredients

3 to 4 ice cubes

¾ measure applejack

¾ measure orange juice

¾ measure lemon juice

¾ measure maple syrup

½ slice orange, to garnish

method

Shake all of the ingredients (apart from the orange garnish) firmly in a shaker, then strain into a cocktail glass. Garnish with ½ slice of orange.

lumberjack

method: mixing glass   **glass:** rocks   **ice:** cubes   **garnish:** lemon twist

The 'jack' in this cocktail's name refers to applejack, the apple brandy that's a speciality of New England. Apple brandy is also made on the west coast of America, but here the producers generally use the French term *eau-de-vie de pomme* with which to distinguish their product.

8 to 10 ice cubes

2 tsps gin

2 tsps Scotch whisky

1 measure Calvados or applejack

thin strip lemon peel, to garnish

Put some ice cubes into a mixing glass and pour in the gin, Scotch and Calvados or applejack. Strain into an ice-filled rocks glass and squeeze the lemon peel over the drink to release the oil, then drop the peel into the glass.

b and c

method: build   **glass:** rocks   **ice:** cubes

The name 'b and c' is a useful mnemonic for the cocktail's ingredients: B(enedictine) and C(alvados), both of which are the proud products of Normandy, France. According to local legend, the *département* of Calvados is said to have taken its name from a galleon of the Spanish Armada that was wrecked on the French coast as it fled from Sir Francis Drake.

ingredients

3 to 4 ice cubes

³/₄ measure Benedictine

³/₄ measure Calvados

method

Put a few ice cubes in a rocks glass. Pour over the Benedictine and the Calvados and stir gently.

normandy

Normandy, France, is the home of Calvados, so it's not surprising that this recipe demands it. This drink is almost a cooler as it has a spiral of lemon peel as a garnish, although it doesn't contain soda water (but you could make it into a long drink if you like).

1 lemon wedge, for rimming

caster sugar, for rimming

3 to 4 ice cubes

³/₄ measure orange juice

2 tsps sugar syrup

1 measure Calvados

1 thin strip lemon peel, twisted, to garnish

Run a wedge of lemon around the rim of a goblet and then dip it into caster sugar. Place some ice cubes into a shaker and pour in the orange juice, sugar syrup and Calvados. Shake and strain into the sugar-rimmed goblet and then add the lemon-peel spiral.

calvados cocktail

method: shaker **glass:** cocktail **ice:** cubes **garnish:** ½ sliced orange (2.

There are a number of versions of this cocktail, and two are given here. The first version is fruity and slightly sweet. The second is also fruity, but a little milder in taste. Try them both in order to identify your favourite. Calvados cocktail 1 is pictured at left.

ingredients

Calvados cocktail 1
3 to 4 ice cubes
1½ measures Calvados
¾ measure grenadine
¾ measure orange juice
1 dash orange bitters

Calvados cocktail 2
3 to 4 ice cubes
¾ measure Calvados
¾ measure Grand Marnier
¾ measure orange juice
½ slice orange, to garnish

method

Shake all of the ingredients (apart from the orange garnish if you are making option number 2) together in a shaker and then strain into a cocktail glass. For option number 2, garnish with 1/2 slice of orange before serving.

apple blossom

The apple blossom is the state flower of Michigan and Arkansas, but this adult equivalent of a 'slurpie' is a variation of the Cognac-based cherry blossom (see page 131). This cocktail uses maple syrup as its sweetener, which is fortunately now widely available outside North America.

1 good scoop crushed ice

1 measure Calvados or applejack

³/₄ measure apple juice

1 tbsp maple syrup

2 tsps lemon juice

1 slice lemon, to garnish

Put a good scoop of crushed ice into a blender and pour in the Calvados or applejack, apple juice, maple syrup and lemon juice. Whizz briefly and pour into a chilled champagne saucer. Garnish with a lemon slice.

apple fizz

method: shaker   **glass:** rocks   **ice:** cubes   **garnish:** lemon slice

First developed during the 1870s, fizzes were traditionally served in the morning, or at midday. You can make a fizz as long – or short – as you like by adding chilled soda water. Only fill your glass half-full of ice, though, or you won't get the fizz from the soda.

ingredients

6 to 8 ice cubes

1 measure applejack or Calvados

1 measure lemon juice

1 measure maple syrup

chilled soda water, as required

1 slice lemon, to garnish

method

Place 2 to 3 ice cubes in a shaker and add all of the ingredients, except for the soda water and lemon slice, and shake. Strain into a rocks glass half-filled with the remaining ice cubes and add the chilled soda water to taste. Garnish with the lemon slice.

bentley

method: mixing glass   **glass:** cocktail   **ice:** cubes

This is a classic medium dry aperitif, as chic and smooth as the motor!

ingredients

3 to 4 ice cubes

1 measure Calvados

1 measure Dubonnet

method

Put the ice cubes in the mixing glass and pour in the Calvados and Dubonnet. Stir then strain into a cocktail glass.

frozen apple

method: blender   **glass:** cocktail   **ice:** crushed

This blender-made cocktail uses apple brandy and half the white of an egg, which gives it a frothy, frosted finish. Don't be alarmed about using egg: it's effectively 'cooked' by the alcohol, but if you prefer, you could leave it out, or even replace it with a dash of orange juice.

ingredients

1 good scoop crushed ice

1 measure applejack or Calvados

1 tbsp sugar

2 tsps lime juice

½ the white of 1 egg

method

Put a good scoop of crushed ice into a blender and add the remaining ingredients. Whizz together until blended, and pour into a chilled cocktail glass.

steeplejack

method: build   **glass:** highball or collins   **ice:** cubes   **garnish:** lemon slice

This is a lovely, tall drink – befitting its name – and very refreshing. It's a cross between the 19th-century fizz and Collins, but very simple to make: just add the applejack, apple juice and chilled soda water to a glass of ice.

6 to 8 ice cubes

1 measure applejack

1½ measures chilled apple juice

1½ measures chilled soda water

1 lemon slice, to garnish

Fill a highball or collins glass with ice cubes, add the remaining ingredients (apart from the lemon slice) and stir gently. Garnish with the lemon slice before serving.

widow's kiss

This must be one of the most luxurious cocktails ever devised: a mix of three of France's finest products: Calvados and Benedictine, from Normandy, and Chartreuse, from the wooded foothills of the Alps near Grenoble. The floating-strawberry garnish is unusual, but delicious!

ingredients

1 good scoop crushed ice

1 measure Calvados

1 measure Benedictine

1/2 measure yellow Chartreuse

1 dash angostura bitters

1 strawberry, to garnish

method

Place a good scoop of crushed ice in a shaker and pour in the Calvados, Benedictine and yellow Chartreuse and add the dash of bitters. Shake well and strain into a chilled cocktail glass. Now float the strawberry garnish on the top.

liberty

The Statue of Liberty, who welcomes all to New York's harbour, was a gift from the French nation to honour American independence. Ladies and gentlemen, raise your glasses: 'To Liberty and *liberté*!

3 to 4 ice cubes

1½ measures Calvados

¾ measure rum

1 dash sugar syrup

Put some ice cubes in a mixing glass and add the remaining ingredients. Mix and strain into a chilled cocktail glass.

big apple

method: mixing glass **glass:** cocktail **ice:** cubes

Most folks know that New York's nickname is 'the Big Apple', but less well-known is the Jazz Age dance, also of that name. Next time you want to cut a dash, try this for size! This drink calls for applejack, which is sometimes known as 'Jersey lightning', after the state in which it is produced.

ingredients

3 to 4 ice cubes

1 measure apple juice

2 tsps brandy

1 measure applejack

method

Put some ice cubes into a mixing glass and pour in the apple juice, brandy and applejack. Stir and strain into a chilled cocktail glass.

eau de vie, akavit & schnaps

Eau de vie ('water of life') is the French term for all brandies. Any grape brandy is brandy, but because Cognac and Armagnac enjoy strict legislation and prestige in France, lesser grape brandies tend to end up overseas. In general, the term 'eaux de vie' applies to fruit brandies that are colourless and have been aged in glass or pottery, and not in wooden barrels. Because of this, they are also sometimes known as 'alcools blancs' ('white alcohols'), and have an alcohol content of 38 to 45 per cent.

Some of the finest eaux de vie are produced in the Alsace region bordering France and Germany, in the Black Forest region of Germany and in northern Switzerland. Every type of fruit is used, but the best-known eaux de vie are those made from cherries, such as Kirsch, from plums (small, sour, blue–purple Switzen plums make the dry white Quetsch, while yellow Mirabelle plums make the fine, white eau de vie), from strawberries (fraise) and from raspberries (framboise). Poire William is made from William's pears (also known as Bartlett pears), largely in Switzerland. The unique point about this eau de vie is that each bottle contains a single pear. The bottles are attached to the trees, so that a pear grows inside each (in its own, mini-greenhouse!), and when both bottle and pear are picked, the remaining space is filled with a fragrant, pear brandy.

Akavit is the name given to the native spirits of Scandinavia, regardless of flavour, although caraway and dill are the most common. Akavit, the spelling common in Denmark, is a neutral spirit distilled from grain and redistilled with flavourings, a little like gin. Danish akavit is said to date from 1846, when a Polish distiller called Isidor Henius set up shop in the Danish town of Aalborg and produced Aalborg Taffel, or 'red Aalborg', after the colour of its label. Akavit is most often served ice cold in small, ice-frosted, shot glasses, but, increasingly, imaginative bartenders are finding that it is a terrific base for new cocktails.

'Schnaps', or 'schnapps', originally meant 'a swallow' or 'a gulp' in German. In Austria, it is often served chilled and neat, and is flavoured with apples and pears (called Obstler), plums or cherries. In Germany, schnaps (spelled with just one 'p') is also often served neat, but is not downed in one. Instead, it is savoured on the tongue! Korn is another type of clear schnaps from German-speaking regions of Europe, and is produced from a variety of grains.

midnight sun

method: shaker   **glass:** champagne saucer   **ice:** cubes   **garnish:** 1/2 slice orange

In the far north of Scandinavia, in the Arctic Circle, the sun is visible at midnight in midsummer. Akavit is usually served ice cold, but here the northern chill is taken off it by the addition of grenadine, a sweet syrup made from pomegranates.

ingredients

3 to 4 ice cubes

2 tsps grapefruit juice

2 tsps lemon juice

2 tsps sugar syrup

2 dashes grenadine

1 measure akavit

1/2 slice orange, to garnish

method

Place some ice cubes in a shaker and pour in the grapefruit juice, lemon juice, sugar syrup, grenadine and akavit. Shake well and strain into a champagne saucer. Garnish with 1/2 slice of orange.

danish dynamite

method: shaker   **glass:** cocktail   **ice:** cubes   **garnish:** ½ slice orange

It was a Polish vodka-distiller called Isidor Henius who, trying his hand at making akavit, produced Aalborg Taffel in 1846. This appropriately named 'Danish dynamite' uses both akavit and vodka, which ideally should be very, very chilled.

ingredients

3 to 4 ice cubes

1½ measures orange juice

1 measure akavit

2 tsps lime juice

½ slice orange, to garnish

method

Shake all of the ingredients, with the exception of the ½ slice of orange, together in a shaker, strain into a cocktail glass and then garnish with the halved orange slice.

time bomb

method: shaker   **glass:** cocktail   **ice:** cubes   **garnish:** lemon peel

The best-known Danish akavit is Aalborg Taffel, affectionately known as 'red Aalborg' after the red details on its label. This distinctive, caraway-flavoured akavit has been made in the town of Aalborg since 1846.

ingredients

3 to 4 ice cubes

³/₄ measure akavit

³/₄ measure vodka

³/₄ measure lemon juice

1 thin strip lemon peel, to garnish

method

Place some ice cubes in a shaker and pour in the remaining ingredients, apart from the lemon peel. Shake and strain into a chilled cocktail glass and sit the piece of lemon peel on the rim.

art

method: build   **glass:** highball or collins   **ice:** cubes   **garnish:** 4 maraschino cherries

This gorgeous, long, refreshing drink is based on Kirsch, a fruit brandy made from cherries in the area where France, Germany and Switzerland meet. Kirsch is the name for a brandy that retains the fruit's flavour, while Kirschwasser ('cherry water') indicates a drier, stronger spirit. The four-cherry garnish is unique to this cocktail.

4 to 6 ice cubes

1 measure Kirsch

³/₄ measure grenadine

chilled soda water, as required

4 maraschino cherries, to garnish

Half-fill a highball or collins glass with ice. Pour in the Kirsch and grenadine and stir gently. Top with chilled soda water and stir briefly. Drop the 4 maraschino cherries into the glass, add a stirrer and serve.

kornelius

The name of this cocktail hints at the main ingredient: korn. This is a clear, grain spirit that originated in Germany's Harz Mountains. Technically, it's a type of schnaps, but it's never downed in one, but is rather savoured on the tongue. Here, the flavour is enhanced by the addition of the two vermouths.

ingredients

3 to 4 ice cubes

1 measure korn (or any flavourless schnaps)

2 tsps dry vermouth

2 tsps sweet, red vermouth

2 tsps grenadine

1 orange slice, to garnish

method

Shake all of the ingredients together, apart from the orange garnish, in a shaker. Strain into a chilled cocktail glass and garnish with the orange slice.

akavit rickey

method: build   **glass:** highball   **ice:** cubes

Rickeys are unsweetened cocktails made of a spirit, lime juice and soda water, and were first made in around 1893 in Shoemaker's Restaurant, Washington, the USA, for Joe Rickey, known as 'Colonel Jim', a Congressional lobbyist.

ingredients

4 to 6 ice cubes

$1/4$ fresh lime

2 measures akavit

1 tsp kümmel

chilled soda water, as required

method

Half-fill a highball glass with ice cubes and squeeze in the lime directly. Drop in the spent lime shell and pour in the akavit and kümmel. Stir and add the chilled soda water.

You can make a rickey with any spirit: simply replace the akavit and kümmel with 2 measures of your preferred spirit.

akatini

method: mixing glass   **glass:** cocktail   **ice:** cubes

This variation on the martini comes from Lysholm Linie, the makers of Norway's premium aquavit. Jorgen B Lysholm, in an attempt to establish an overseas market, sent some potato spirit to the East Indies in 1805. This meant a sea journey across the Equator – this is the 'line' (*linie* in Norwegian) in the name – and back because the spirit didn't sell, but the sea voyage vastly improved the flavour!

ingredients

3 to 4 ice cubes

1 dash Noilly Prat

1½ measures Lysholm Linie aquavit

method

Place some ice cubes in a mixing glass and pour in the Noilly Prat and the aquavit. Stir briefly and strain into a well-chilled cocktail glass.

the viking

Ever since Mr Lysholm sent his spirit on its first sea trip, Lysholm Linie aquavit has been aged for four-and-a-half months on a world cruise. On the label of each bottle is the date of the cruise and the name of the ship! This recipe, courtesy of Lysholm Linie, makes use of tropical fruits that the aquavit would have passed as it crossed the Equator.

6 ice cubes

1 measure pineapple juice

1 measure white Curaçao

1 measure Lysholm Linie aquavit

Put 6 ice cubes in a shaker and pour over the pineapple juice, white Curaçao and aquavit. Shake well and strain into a cocktail glass.

grand quetsch

method: mixing glass · · · · · **glass:** cocktail · · · · · **ice:** crushed · · · · · **garnish:** orange slice

Quetsch (or *Zwetschenwasser*) is one of the world's great eaux de vie. It is distilled from the small, sour, deep-purple quetsch, or Switzer plum, to make a dry, white eau de vie. The 'grand' in the name comes from Grand Marnier, the fine, Cognac-based, orange liqueur from France.

ingredients

1 measure Grand Marnier

1 tsp Quetsch

1 tsp orange juice

1 scoop crushed ice

1 orange slice, to garnish

method

Pour the Grand Marnier, Quetsch and orange juice into a mixing glass and stir. Pour over crushed ice in a cocktail glass and garnish with an orange slice.

dorchester golden fizz

method: shaker   **glass:** highball   **ice:** cubes

This wonderful, long drink was devised by Guilio Morandin at the Dorchester Hotel, in London's Park Lane. Schnaps has become increasing available in a wide range of flavours for cocktail use: there is apple, cherry, peppermint, cinnamon, blackberry and even banana butterscotch! This cocktail uses peach schnaps.

8 to 10 ice cubes

1 ½ tbsps lemon juice

1 tsp sugar syrup

½ measure peach schnaps

1 measure white rum

dash of egg white

chilled lemonade, as required

Put half of the ice in a shaker and pour in the lemon juice, sugar syrup, peach schnaps and white rum. Add a dash of egg white and shake vigorously to froth up the mix. Strain into a highball glass half-filled with the remaining ice. Top up with chilled lemonade.

silver bullet

method: mixing glass **glass:** cocktail **ice:** cubes

This classic cocktail makes use of vodka and kümmel, a liqueur made with caraway, cumin, fennel, oris and a host of other herbs. Originally, kümmel was made in the late 16th century by Lucas Bols in Amsterdam, and was taken by the Russian tsar, Peter the Great (who was working incognito as a labourer in the Dutch shipyards), to the distillery at Allasch Castle, near Riga in Latvia.

ingredients

3 to 4 ice cubes

1 measure kümmel

1 1/2 measures vodka

method

Place some ice cubes in a mixing glass and add the kümmel and vodka. Stir briefly and strain into a cocktail glass.

flashing fizz

method: shaker   **glass:** highball or collins   **ice:** cubes

Switzerland is renowned for its Kirsch, for the country is the world's largest producer of cherries! Kirsch is made here with the dark, nearly black, 'mountain cherries', the finest of which grow at the very top of the cherry trees, although connoisseurs insist that Kirsch made with wild cherries is the finer of the two. This fizz also uses crème de cassis, a blackcurrant liqueur that is a speciality of the Dijon region of France.

8 to 10 ice cubes

1 measure Kirsch

1/2 measure crème de cassis

chilled, sparkling mineral water, as required

Put half of the ice in a shaker and pour in the Kirsch and crème de cassis. Shake and strain into a highball or collins glass half-filled with the remaining ice. Top with sparkling mineral water.

rosalind russell

method: mixing glass   **glass:** cocktail   **ice:** cubes

The Hollywood movie star for whom this drink is named was, in fact, born in Denmark, so it's no surprise that this caraway-flavoured cocktail should use Danish akavit like 'red Aalborg'. The second ingredient is red vermouth, the commercial production of which was begun in Turin, Italy, during the 18th century, by Carlo and Giovanno Cinzano, although the ancient Egyptians were among the first to 'fortifty' and flavour wine.

ingredients

3 to 4 ice cubes

2 measures Danish akavit

1 measure red vermouth

1 thin strip lemon peel

method

Stir the ingredients, apart from the lemon peel, together in a mixing glass and then strain into a chilled cocktail glass. Twist the lemon peel over the glass to release the citrus oil, and then discard it.

korn sour

method: shaker　　　**glass:** rocks　　　**ice:** cubes　　　**garnish:** maraschino cherry

Sours are the simplest of the classic mixed drinks, and are made of a spirit, citrus and sugar. As the name implies, they should never taste sweet, but you can adjust the sugar to suit your preference. This sour makes use of korn, a type of schnaps produced from a variety of grains. There is also doppel korn, literally 'double grain', which is distilled from wheat.

8 to 10 ice cubes

2 tsps sugar syrup

³/₄ measure lemon juice

1¹/₂ measures korn or another schnaps

chilled, sparkling mineral water (optional)

1 maraschino cherry, to garnish

Put 3 to 4 ice cubes in a shaker and pour in the sugar syrup, lemon juice and korn. Shake well and strain into a rocks glass half-filled with the remaining ice. Top with chilled, sparkling mineral water if you like, and then finally garnish with a maraschino cherry.

poire william &
bitter lemon

This simple, long drink uses Poire William, an aromatic eau de vie distilled from Williams pears. Also known as Williamine, in each bottle of the eau de vie is a single fruit that has been grown in its own little greenhouse! If you've never tried Poire William, this fruity, tangy mix is a great introduction.

ingredients

3 to 4 ice cubes

1 ½ measures Poire William

chilled bitter lemon, as required

1 pear wedge, to garnish

method

Put some ice into a highball or collins glass and pour in the Poire William. Top up with chilled bitter lemon and garnish with the pear wedge.

danish mary

This is but one variation of the famous bloody Mary invented in 1921 by Fernand, 'Pete' Petiot, of Harry's Bar in Paris, which was supposedly named after the Hollywood star Mary Pickford. This Danish Mary naturally uses Danish akavit, but Mary does travel well: use korn, and she's a German Mary; tequila, and she's a bloody Maria; while a non-alcoholic version is, of course, a virgin Mary.

3 to 4 ice cubes

3½ measures tomato juice

2 tsps lemon juice

¾ measure Danish akavit

freshly ground black pepper

celery salt

2 dashes Worcestershire sauce.

1 stick celery

Place some ice cubes in a shaker and pour in the tomato juice, lemon juice and akavit. Season to taste (if you want a spicier taste, add a drop of hot pepper sauce!) Strain into a highball or collins glass, over ice if you like, and garnish with a celery stick.

For a German Mary, substitute korn or another flavourless schnaps for the akavit.

bitters & fortified wines

The meaning of the word 'bitters' is wide-ranging, and is used to describe both bitter essences and alcoholic drinks made from roots, flowers, fruits and their peels, macerated in a neutral spirit. Bitters are valued for their appetite-stimulating and digestion-promoting qualities.

The most famous patented bitters are angostura (45 per cent alcohol by volume, or abv). These were originally made in the town of Angostura, in Venezuela, but are now produced in Trinidad. The recipe was formulated in 1824 by a military doctor, according to a 'secret formula'. The exact recipe remains a closely guarded secret, but gentian is the most pronounced ingredient, along with extracts of Seville orange peel, angelica, cardamon, cinnamon, cloves, quinine and galagan (*Alpinia officinarum*). Angostura bitters are an indispensable element of the bar – just a few dashes turn Plymouth gin into a pink gin, but those little drops of bitters also have the capacity to add sweetness to a sour drink and sharpness to a sweet drink. In addition to angostura bitters, there are also Peychaud bitters (Franco–American bitters) and Underberg bitters from Germany, which have been brewed to a secret family recipe since 1846 and claim to be a cure for hangovers!

'Bitters' is also the word used to describe such bitter apéritifs and *digestifs* as Amer Picon (21 per cent abv), from France, and Campari (24 per cent abv), from Italy.

Amaro is the Italian word for bitters, and it is used to describe the many (over five hundred) patented, bitter liqueurs produced in that country. Amaros, which are usually dark brown in colour, are made from herbs, plants and tree barks, which are diluted and served with ice as apéritifs, or are served neat as *digestifs*.

Fortified wines are all ordinary wines that have been fortified with another form of alcohol: port, sherry and vermouth are all fortified wines. Port (from Portugal) is fortified by adding local brandy during the grape fermentation. Doing so prevents the grapes from fermenting completely, which results in the sweetness of the wine.

Sherry derives its name from the English people's inability to pronounce the Spanish name Jerez! This wine is also fortified with brandy.

Vermouth is a fortified wine, too, which is flavoured with herbs, barks and plant extracts. Although produced mainly in France and Italy, the word 'vermouth' comes from the German *Wermut*, meaning 'wormwood', although none of the health scares that affected absinthe seem to have troubled vermouth.

rose water

method: build   **glass:** highball   **ice:** cubes

This simple, yet refreshing, tall drink is made using the Italian patented apéritif Campari, which is very dry and has a quite pronounced, quinine taste. Manufactured from a combination of herbs, spices, fruit and barks, Campari was first made in 1862, by Gaspare Campari.

3 to 4 ice cubes

1 tsp grenadine

½ measure Campari

6 measures chilled lemonade

Put some ice into a highball glass. Pour in the grenadine and the Campari and top with the chilled lemonade.

the manager's daughte

This citrus-wine-flavoured drink uses Dubonnet, France's vermouth-style apéritif. Fortified wine dates back to the ancient Egyptians, but the Romans were the first to include wormwood. These wines became popular in Germany during the 16th century (the German word for wormwood is *Wermut*), and later at the French royal court, where their name became vermouth.

ingredients

3 to 4 ice cubes

1 measure apple brandy

1 ½ measures Dubonnet

4 measures sparkling bitter lemon

1 lemon slice, to garnish

method

Put some ice cubes in a highball glass and pour in the apple brandy and the Dubonnet. Stir briefly, then top with sparkling bitter lemon and garnish with a lemon slice.

silver campari

method: shaker   **glass:** champagne flute   **ice:** cubes

According to legend, Gaspare Campari created his rich-red-coloured apéritif in the basement of his café-bar in Milan's fashionable Galleria in 1862, and it soon became a most fashionable drink. Even a papal warrant was issued, and Campari was consequently served in the Vatican.

3 to 4 ice cubes

³/₄ measure Campari

³/₄ measure gin

1 measure lemon juice

2 tsps sugar syrup

sparkling white wine or champagne, as required

1 thin strip lemon peel

Shake all of the ingredients (except for the sparkling wine or champagne and the lemon peel) in a shaker. Strain into a champagne flute and top with the sparkling wine or champagne. Twist the lemon peel over the drink to release its oil, and then discard it.

campola

method: build   **glass:** highball   **ice:** cubes   **garnish:** lime slice & maraschino cherry

This is another glorious drink that takes its name from its ingredients: Campari and cola. There is, however, also just a little sweet (oloroso) sherry, a rich, dark and very versatile, fortified (with brandy) wine when used in making cocktails.

ingredients

3 to 4 ice cubes

1 measure Campari

½ measure sweet sherry

5 measures cold cola

1 lime slice, to garnish

1 maraschino cherry, to garnish

method

Put some ice cubes in a highball glass and add the Campari and sherry and top with the cola. Garnish with 1 lime slice and 1 maraschino cherry and serve with a straw.

174 bitters & fortified wines

negroni

Cocktail lore says that this drink was devised by Count Negroni. It is a variation on the famous americano – a mix of Campari and sweet, Italian vermouth – but with gin in place of soda water.

3 to 4 ice cubes

2 measures gin

1 measure sweet, Italian vermouth

1 measure Campari

1 orange slice, to garnish

Put the ice into a goblet and pour over the gin, vermouth and Campari. Stir well and then drop in 1 orange slice.

savoy sangaree

The sangaree is a 19th-century, American mix influenced by the traditional Spanish red-wine-based drink called sangria. Originally, it was a sweetened, fortified wine served in a tumbler. During the early 20th century, soda water was added to the sangaree. Sangarees can be made with fortified wines or spirits, and are traditionally dusted with nutmeg. This version, as its name suggests, is the recipe from London's famous Savoy Hotel.

ingredients

3 to 4 ice cubes

1 tsp caster sugar

1 large glass port or sherry

1 scoop broken ice

1 orange slice, to garnish

grated nutmeg, to garnish

method

Put some ice cubes in a mixing glass and pour in the sugar and port or sherry. Stir well and strain into a rocks glass half-filled with broken ice. Garnish with 1 orange slice and a dusting of grated nutmeg. Serve with a straw.

first avenue

method: build   **glass:** rocks   **ice:** broken

Avenues are a class of drinks based on sweet sherry and built in a very cold glass. A fruit liqueur is also used – in this instance, orange-flavoured Cointreau – to make a subtle contribution to the overall flavour.

1 scoop broken ice

1 ½ measures sweet sherry

½ measure Cointreau

1 tsp Campari

¾ measure soda water

Put some broken ice into a rocks glass and pour in the sherry, Cointreau and Campari. Top with soda water.

Take a stroll down Second Avenue and replace the Cointreau with ½ measure of peach schnaps, or down Third Avenue, and replace it with ½ measure of melon liqueur.

ferrari cocktail

method: mixing glass   **glass:** cocktail   **ice:** cubes

This cocktail is a spicy mix of dry vermouth and one of Italy's most famous liqueurs, the amber-coloured, almond-flavoured amaretto, which is first said to have been made in Saronno in 1525. An extra bite is added by the oil released from the grated lemon zest.

ingredients

3 to 4 ice cubes

grated peel of ½ lemon

1¼ measures dry vermouth

¾ measure amaretto

method

Put the ice into a mixing glass and add the grated lemon peel, vermouth and amaretto. Stir and then strain into a cocktail glass.

southern tango

The 'southern' in the name of this cocktail indicates the inclusion of America's strong, dry, bourbon-and-peach liqueur, Southern Comfort. Here, it is complemented by a pale-golden and dry-white-wine-based vermouth that, in France, is traditionally aged in oak vats.

I scoop broken ice

I measure dry vermouth

$^1/_2$ measure Southern Comfort

2 measures chilled lemonade

Into a highball glass two-thirds filled with broken ice, pour the vermouth and Southern Comfort. Then top with the chilled lemonade.

bitters & fortified wines **179**

campus

method: mixing glass   **glass:** rocks   **ice:** cubes   **garnish:** orange segment

Orange is the typical garnish for drinks made with Campari as it complements the Seville-orange peel used in its production. The subtle smokiness of Scotch, and the botanicals in the gin, make for a very interesting mix.

ingredients

3 to 4 ice cubes

1 ³/₄ measures Campari

¹/₄ measure Scotch whisky

2 tsps gin

1 orange segment, to garnish

method

Place half of the ice in a mixing glass and add the remaining ingredients, apart from the orange segment. Stir and strain into a rocks glass filled with the rest of the ice. Finally, drop the orange segment into the glass.

trocadero

This medium-dry cocktail uses dry, white vermouth and sweet, red vermouth, as well as a dash of angostura bitters, a gentian-flavoured tincture originally made in 1824, in the town of Angostura (now Cuidad Bolívar), in Venezuela, by Dr Johann Siegert, a German army surgeon in Simon Bolivar's Liberation Army. Originally a medicine, angostura bitters is today an essential item in any well-stocked bar.

3 to 4 ice cubes

1 measure dry, white vermouth

1 measure sweet, red vermouth

1 dash grenadine

1 dash angostura bitters

1 maraschino cherry, to garnish

Put the ice in a mixing glass and add the remaining ingredients, except for the cherry garnish. Stir and strain into a cocktail glass. To finish, garnish with 1 maraschino cherry.

diplomat

method: mixing glass   **glass:** rocks   **ice:** cubes & broken   **garnish:** maraschino cherry

This 1920s' cocktail classic was originally served straight up, but is now more popular on the rocks as an apéritif. It includes a small amount of maraschino, a distinctive, colourless, cherry liqueur originally made in Dalmatia, but now largely produced in Italy.

ingredients

3 to 4 ice cubes

2 measures dry vermouth

$^2/_3$ measure red vermouth

1 tsp maraschino

1 scoop broken ice

1 maraschino cherry, to garnish

method

Place the ice cubes in a mixing glass and add the remaining ingredients, except for the broken ice and cherry garnish. Stir and strain into a rocks glass two-thirds filled with broken ice. Garnish with a maraschino cherry on a stick.

port flip

method: shaker   **glass:** champagne flute   **ice:** cubes   **garnish:** grated nutmeg

Originating in the 17th century, flips take their name from the original method of mixing them: they were flipped back and forth from one vessel to another in order to obtain a smooth mix. Today, we don't have to be so dextrous – simply use a shaker to create a perfect, creamy cocktail.

3 to 4 ice cubes

1 ¹/₂ measures port

2 tsps Cognac

1 tsp sugar syrup

1 egg yolk

grated nutmeg, to garnish

Place all of the ingredients, except for the nutmeg, in a shaker and shake firmly. Strain into a champagne flute and sprinkle a little grated nutmeg over the top.

mermaid

method: build   **glass:** highball   **ice:** cubes   **garnish:** orange slice & lemon peel

When blue Curaçao was developed during the 1960s, cocktail bartenders the world over vied with each other to create new recipes that included it. Curaçao takes its name from the Caribbean island that is famed for its small, bitter oranges of the same name. It was the Dutch who originally produced the clear, colourless, orange-flavoured liqueur, which is now available in a range of vivid hues.

ingredients

3 to 4 ice cubes

³/₄ measure sweet, white vermouth

³/₄ measure gin

³/₄ measure blue Curaçao

chilled bitter orange, as required

1 slice orange, to garnish

1 thin strip lemon peel, twisted, to garnish

method

Put some ice cubes into a highball glass and pour in the white vermouth, gin and blue Curaçao. Stir together, then top with the bitter orange and stir gently once more. Garnish with 1 orange slice and 1 lemon-peel spiral. Add a straw if you like.

bahia cocktail

method: mixing glass　　**glass:** cocktail　　**ice:** cubes

The rather dusty, dry image of sherry means that it is overlooked by many as a first choice for drinks. Fortunately, a number of inventive barmen have created some seriously delicious cocktails using sherry as the base wine. If you like your drinks a little spicy, and with a sharp tang, then this is for you!

6 to 8 ice cubes

1 measure medium sherry

1 measure dry vermouth

2 dashes pastis or Pernod

1 dash angostura bitters

1 thin strip lemon peel

Put plenty of ice in a mixing glass and add all of the remaining ingredients, except for the lemon peel. Mix, then strain into a chilled cocktail glass. Twist the lemon peel over the drink to release the oil, then discard it.

liqueur cocktails

The word 'liqueur' means different things to different people: to the French, it is any after-dinner drink, such as liqueur brandy. To the British, a liqueur is a sweetish drink made from a base spirit into which flavouring agents, such as roots, fruits, seeds, barks and flowers, have been infused, macerated or redistilled. In the United States, liqueurs are called cordials (a word that, in Britain, means a flavoured syrup, with little or no alcohol in it).

Liqueurs are among the oldest forms of alcoholic drinks. Monks in religious fraternities worked with herbs to exploit their medicinal properties and were among the first to produce liqueurs. They achieved this by adding honey or sugar to sweeten the bitter elixirs that they were making for their patients. Two of the most famous of these 'holy elixirs' are Chartreuse and Benedictine. Chartreuse, made originally by Carthusian monks at the monastery of La Grande Chartreuse, near Grenoble, France, dates back to the early 16th century and contains 130 herbs and spices. The maceration, infusion and distillation process was perfected in 1764, and commercial production began in 1848. When, at one stage, the monks were exiled to Spain, they began a distillery in Tarragona. The distillery is visited three times each year by the only three monks who, at any one time, know the secret recipe. There are two forms of Chartreuse: a mild yellow Chartreuse and a spicier, and more powerful, green Chartreuse.

Benedictine is often described as the world's oldest liqueur as it dates from 1510. The amber-coloured liqueur originated in the abbey at Fécamp in Normandy, northern France. The abbey was sacked during the French Revolution, and, in 1863, the secret formula passed into the hands of a local merchant called Alexander Le Grand, said to be a descendent of a trustee of the abbey. Le Grand recreated the elixir, which contains 27 herbs, plants, flowers and fruit peels, and each bottle is still emblazoned with the motto *Deo Optimo Maximo* ('To God Most Good, Most Great').

Liqueurs come in an enormous range of flavours, from mint to chocolate, and from nut to coffee, as well as containing practically every fruit under the sun. Some of the most frequently used in cocktails are those called 'crème'. In spite of their name, they do not usually contain cream, but consist mostly of Cognac or brandy, plus the flavour. There is, for instance, crème de banane (banana); crème de cacao (chocolate, available in light and dark versions), crème de menthe (mint, available in white or green hues), crème de cassis (blackcurrant), fraise (strawberry), and framboise (raspberry).

galliano stinger

Very refreshing and spicy drinks, stingers were originally served straight up, but during the Prohibition in the USA, they became popular served over crushed ice. It's the crème de menthe that provides the 'sting' in this Galliano-based mix, a liqueur that rose to fame in the harvey wallbanger during the 1950s.

2 to 3 ice cubes

1½ measures Galliano

¾ measure white crème de menthe

1 scoop crushed ice (optional)

Put some ice cubes in a shaker, add the Galliano and white crème de menthe and shake. Strain into a cocktail glass if you want it straight up, or strain over crushed ice in a champagne saucer.

Try these other stingers:

comfortable stinger: 1½ measures Southern Comfort;

roman stinger: ¾ measure sambuca and ¾ measure Cognac;

bee stinger: 1½ measures blackberry brandy.

lost bikini

method: shaker   **glass:** cocktail   **ice:** cubes   **garnish:** 2 cherries

The two cherries in the garnish say it all! A cool, sweet drink, ideal for summer evenings lounging on the beach or by the pool. If neither of these are available, just sit back and use your imagination.

ingredients

3 to 4 ice cubes

³/₄ measure Galliano

³/₄ measure amaretto

¹/₂ measure white rum

¹/₂ measure lime juice

2 measures mandarin juice

2 cherries, to garnish

method

Place all of the ingredients, except for the cherries, in a shaker and shake. Strain into a cocktail glass and then garnish with the 2 cherries.

b-52

4 to 6 ice cubes

1 measure Kahlua or Tia
Maria

1 measure Baileys Irish Cream

1 measure Grand Marnier

Variations:

1 measure Tia Maria or Kahlua

1 measure amaretto

1 measure Baileys Irish Cream

1 measure Cointreau

1 measure Baileys Irish Cream

1 measure Tia Maria

2 measures amaretto

1 measure absinthe

1 measure dark rum

This well-known drink has become popular with younger drinkers as a shooter, in which the different ingredients are layered in a glass. You can also serve them stirred and strained into an ice-filled rocks glass. The B-52's popularity has also given rise to numerous subtle variations, so you can make your favourite combination.

Pour the ingredients slowly over the back of a bar spoon, and in the order given, so that they lie in layers, one on top of the other. Alternatively, mix the ingredients in a mixing glass with ice and strain into an ice-filled rocks glass.

hollywood nuts

Rum and two types of nuts are evident here: hazelnuts, from the amber-coloured Frangelico, and almonds, from the amaretto. Here, they are mixed with dark crème de cacao – chocolate-flavoured, with just a hint of vanilla.

ingredients

6 to 8 ice cubes

¹/₂ measure amaretto

¹/₂ measure dark crème de cacao

¹/₂ measure Frangelico

I measure white rum

I tsp egg white

I measure chilled lemonade

method

Put 2 to 3 ice cubes in a shaker and pour in the liqueurs, the rum and the egg white. Shake well and then strain into a rocks glass filled with the remaining ice cubes. Finally, top with the chilled lemonade.

mandarin

This is a very exotic cocktail, for it makes use of Benedictine (said to be the oldest liqueur in the world), Galliano, Cointreau and Mandarine Napoleon. The first two ingredients give the mix its herbal tones, while the last two ingredients give the drink its delicate, orange flavour.

1 glassful crushed ice

1/2 measure Benedictine

1/3 measure Galliano

2/3 measure apricot brandy

2/3 measure triple sec or Cointreau

1 tsp Mandarine Napoleon

1 measure double cream

1 measure orange juice

1 orange slice, to garnish

1 cherry, to garnish

Put the crushed ice in a blender and add all of the remaining ingredients, except for the fruit garnishes. Blend together briefly, then pour into a large cocktail glass. Garnish with 1 orange slice and 1 cherry, both speared on a cocktail stick.

pink squirrel

method: shaker **glass:** champagne saucer **ice:** cubes **garnish:** flaked almonds

The 'pink' in the name of this creamy drink is provided by the grenadine, while the 'squirrel' is a reference to nuts, in this case, the almond flavour of the amaretto and the garnish of flaked almonds. The second flavour evident here is chocolate, so if you have a sweet tooth, this is definitely one for you!

ingredients

1 wedge lemon, for rimming

caster sugar, for rimming

3 to 4 ice cubes

1 ½ measures white crème de cacao

1 ½ measures amaretto

1 measure double cream

¼ measure grenadine

flaked almonds, to garnish

method

Rub the rim of a champagne saucer with the lemon wedge and then dip it into the caster sugar. Put some ice cubes in a shaker and then pour in the remaining ingredients, except for the flaked almonds. Shake well, strain into the sugar-rimmed glass and sprinkle a few flaked almonds on top.

dizzy blonde

method: build   **glass:** goblet   **ice:** broken   **garnish: lemon** slice & green cocktail cherry

This is a great way to enjoy the Dutch brandy-and-egg liqueur, advocaat. The name of Warninks is synonymous with advocaat, and the company reputedly breaks 18,000 eggs each hour to make this, often overlooked, liqueur. In the Netherlands, there are two styles readily available: a thick version, eaten with a spoon and a biscuit, and a thinner version, now popularly drunk on the rocks and with a mixer. Lucky German drinkers can also enjoy mocha-and-chocolate-flavoured advocaat.

I scoop broken ice

I measure orange juice

2 measures advocaat

³/₄ measure Pernod

2 measures chilled lemonade

I lemon slice, to garnish

I green cocktail cherry, to garnish

Put some broken ice into a goblet (or large wine glass) and pour in the orange juice, advocaat and Pernod. Stir briefly to mix, and then top with chilled lemonade. Garnish with I lemon slice and I green cocktail cherry.

midori sour

method: shaker   **glass:** rocks   **ice:** cubes & broken   **garnish:** lemon twist

The sour was invented during the 1850s, but it took another century or so for the Japanese distiller Sun-Tory to develop its bright-green, melon liqueur called Midori.

ingredients

2 to 3 ice cubes

1½ measures Midori

1 measure lemon juice

½ measure sugar syrup

1 scoop broken ice

1 thin strip lemon peel, twisted, to garnish

chilled soda water (optional)

method

Put the ice cubes in a shaker and add the Midori, lemon juice and sugar syrup. Shake and then strain into a rocks glass two-thirds full of broken ice. Garnish with the lemon peel, twisted to make a spiral. Top with a splash of soda water if you wish.

Try a raspberry sour: use 1½ measures Chambord and ½ measure white rum; *for an amaretto sour,* use 1½ measures amaretto.

wobbly knee

method: blender   **glass:** large cocktail   **ice:** crushed   **garnish:** grated chocolate

This is a delicious, almond- and coffee-flavoured cocktail with a hint of coconut. Coconut cream is available ready made, but it's easy to make your own. What might have become a very sweet drink is 'cut' by the addition of the small amount of vodka.

I good scoop crushed ice

I measure amaretto

I measure Kahlua

$^1/_2$ measure vodka

$^3/_4$ measure coconut cream

I measure double cream

grated chocolate, to garnish

Place all of the ingredients, except for the chocolate, in a blender and blend briefly. Pour, unstrained, into a large cocktail glass and sprinkle grated chocolate over the top.

white christmas

method: shaker **glass:** cocktail **ice:** cubes **garnish:** grated chocolate

This whisky-flavoured, creamy confection has chocolate and banana undertones. Crème de banane is a golden-yellow-coloured liqueur made from ripe, aromatic bananas. A delicious version is made in Spain's Canary Islands, and comes in a wonderfully kitschy bottle shaped like a bunch of bananas!

ingredients

3 to 4 ice cubes

1 measure crème de banane

1 measure white crème de cacao

1 measure Scotch whisky

1 measure double cream

grated chocolate, to garnish

method

Shake all of the ingredients, except for the chocolate, in a shaker. Strain into a cocktail glass and sprinkle grated chocolate over the top.

barnaby's buffalo blizzard

method: blender   **glass:** collins   **ice:** cubes   **garnish:** maraschino cherry

In 1997, a truly immense blizzard struck the eastern-seaboard states of the United States. Some lucky victims found themselves marooned for three days in heaven – Barnaby's Restaurant in Buffalo – where the time was spent very sensibly: by inventing new cocktails! This recipe was the among the best.

4 to 6 ice cubes

1 measure white crème de cacao

1 measure Galliano

³⁄₄ measure vodka

2 measures milk

1 tsp grenadine

2 tbsps vanilla ice cream

1¹⁄₂ measures whipped cream

1 maraschino cherry, to garnish

Put the ice in a blender with all of the remaining ingredients, except for the whipped cream and maraschino cherry. Blend briefly, then pour, unstrained, into a collins glass and top with whipped cream and the maraschino cherry.

big toe

There are so many gorgeous liqueurs in this drink that it's likely that your big toe will be the last responsive part of your body, so make sure that you're sitting comfortably! It's a great opportunity to make use of Frangelico, a hazelnut-flavoured liqueur said to have been first made in 1650, by a religious recluse called Fra Angelico, by the river Po, in Italy.

ingredients

3 to 4 ice cubes

½ measure Frangelico

½ measure amaretto

½ measure Kahlua

½ measure Baileys Irish Cream

½ measure white rum

½ measure dark crème de cacao

1 maraschino cherry, to garnish

method

Put some ice cubes in a mixing glass and pour in the liquid ingredients. Strain into a liqueur glass and, finally, garnish with a marashino cherry on a stick.

grasshopper

method: shaker   **glass:** champagne saucer   **ice:** cubes   **garnish:** grated chocolate & mint sprig

This vivid-green drink is a blend of whipped cream, chocolate and mint – the perfect after-dinner combination. The word *Chouao* on the label of crème de cacao indicates that the cocoa beans that were used to make the product came from Venezuela, Chouao being a suburb of the city of Caracas.

3 to 4 ice cubes

1 ¹/₃ measures white crème de cacao

1 measure green crème de menthe

1 ¹/₃ measures whipping cream

grated chocolate, to garnish

1 mint sprig, to garnish

Put the ice in a shaker and pour over the crème de cacao, crème de menthe and the cream. Shake vigorously and strain into a champagne saucer. Garnish with some grated chocolate and 1 mint sprig.

For a flying grasshopper, use 1 measure white crème de cacao, 1 measure vodka and ¹/₃ measure green crème de menthe. Shake briefly with ³/₄ glassful of crushed ice and pour, unstrained, into a rocks glass. Add a short straw.

velvet hammer

There are several versions of this drink currently in circulation. Her
are two variations to try. Both are delicious. What they both share
Cointreau and a coffee-flavoured liqueur, the best known of which a
Kahlua, from Mexico, and Tia Maria, from Jamaica.

ingredients

Velvet hammer 1
3 to 4 ice cubes
³/₄ measure Tia Maria or Kahlua
³/₄ measure Cointreau
³/₄ measure single cream

Velvet hammer 2
3 to 4 ice cubes
1 measure Tia Maria or Kahlua
1 measure Cointreau
¹/₂ measure brandy
1 measure whipping cream
1 scoop broken ice
1 cherry, to garnish

method

To make velvet hammer 1, shake the ingredients in a shaker and strain into a cocktail glass.

For a velvet hammer 2, put some ice cubes in a shaker and add all of the remaining ingredients, except for the broken ice and cherry garnish. Shake and strain into a rocks glass filled with broken ice. Garnish with the cherry.

gemini

This orange-Cognac-flavoured drink uses Grand Marnier, which makes use of Caribbean bitter oranges steeped in Cognac. There are two varieties available: the clear Grand Marnier used here, and a red variety called Grand Marnier Cordon Rouge. Also in the mix is the flowery, yet spicy, herbal liqueur Galliano.

1 scoop broken ice

1 measure chilled orange juice

½ measure Cognac

¾ measure Grand Marnier

¾ measure Galliano

1 strip orange peel

Fill a rocks glass two-thirds full of broken ice and pour in the orange juice, Cognac, Grand Marnier and Galliano. Stir briefly, and then twist the strip of orange peel over the drink to release its oil before discarding it.

zipper

Coffee is the traditional post-prandial drink, but a coffee-flavoured cocktail makes a pleasant alternative. This cocktail uses Kahlua, the coffee liqueur from Mexico, along with Baileys Irish Cream, a distinctive, chocolate-flavoured, whiskey-and-double-cream liqueur that was first formulated during the 1970s, and that has enjoyed considerable success ever since.

ingredients

3 to 4 ice cubes

1½ measures Kahlua

1½ measures white rum

1 measure double cream

2 tsps Baileys Irish Cream

grated chocolate, to garnish

method

Place some ice cubes in a shaker and pour in the remaining ingredients, except for the chocolate. Shake well and strain into a cocktail glass. Sprinkle with grated chocolate.

anis cocktails

'Anis' is the word used to cover all drinks that are aniseed-flavoured, but more specifically, it refers to liqueurs of different degrees of sweetness. The best-known anis drinks are absinthe, pastis, raki (and arak), ouzo (sometimes also called douzico) and sambuca, and there are a number of very well-known proprietary brands, such as Ricard and Pernod. In addition, there is anisette, an aniseed-flavoured liqueur from France, the best-known producer of which is a firm called Marie Brizard.

Absinthe, at around 68 per cent alcohol by volume (abv), is often called the 'green muse' and the 'green goddess', the former because it was a popular drink among such French Impressionist painters as Degas and Toulouse-Lautrec and their models, and the latter because of its reputed qualities as an aphrodisiac. Although it is often associated with France, absinthe is, in fact, a 'native' of Switzerland.

By the beginning of the 20th century, absinthe had been banned in most European countries on the grounds that it endangered health: its main ingredient, wormwood (*Artemisia absinthium*, which gives the drink its name), was reputed to cause madness and death. Despite the ban, absinthe continued to be produced illegally in Switzerland and legally in Spain. In large doses, wormwood is indeed a hallucinogen, but its detrimental effects on health, beyond excessive alcohol intake, have not, so far, been proven. In recent years, the ban on absinthe has been lifted and it is now possible to buy it once more.

To replace the banned absinthe, anis drinks of around 45 per cent abv were introduced. These drinks are typified by Pernod, and by such pastis as that produced by Ricard. The new drinks replaced the wormwood of absinthe with star anise, the fruit of the evergreen, Chinese star-anise tree. The name 'pastis' is derived from the French word for 'a mixture', being 'a pastiche' of ingredients. Pastis has a slightly stronger liquorice flavour than Pernod; it has a brownish tinge when neat, and is paler than Pernod when diluted with water. Drinks of this type, including ouzo and raki, are commonly diluted with four or five parts of water, over ice, which turns the liquor a milky white. The resulting 'colour' has given Pernod is its nicknames of 'tiger's milk' and the 'green fairy'.

Sambuca (approximately 40 per cent abv) is related to the sweet anis liqueurs of France and Spain, but is drier, and its distinctive ingredient is derived from the elder bush. Anisette (around 30 per cent abv) should not be confused with pastis or Pernod: as well as having a lower abv, anisette is a sweet liqueur made by macerating 16 different seeds – including aniseed – fennel, cloves, coriander and other spices and plants, and then blending the maceration with a neutral spirit and sugar syrup.

ladies' cocktail

In spite of its rather delicate-sounding name, this cocktail certainly packs a punch, thanks to its mix of bourbon and Pernod. A more pronounced anis flavour is provided by the anisette, a bitter liqueur made by the firm of Marie Brizzard, which was founded in 1755, in Bordeaux, France.

ingredients

3 to 4 ice cubes

1 ½ measures bourbon

½ tsp Pernod

½ tsp anisette

2 dashes angostura bitters

1 piece pineapple, to garnish

method

Place all of the ingredients, apart from the pineapple, in a mixing glass and stir well. Strain into a cocktail glass and garnish with a piece of pineapple.

hemingway

method: build   **glass:** champagne flute

Created by the American novelist Ernest Hemingway, he mockingly called this drink 'death in the afternoon' and offered the recipe to *Esquire* magazine, with the instructions to drink three or five slowly!

1½ measures absinthe

chilled champagne, as required

Pour the absinthe into the bottom of a champagne flute and then pour in chilled champagne until the mix become milky.

bunny hug

method: shaker   **glass:** cocktail   **ice:** cubes

The bunny hug was a very fast, syncopated dance of the 1920s' Jazz Age. This cocktail combines the Prohibition-era cocktail favourites of gin and whisky with pastis. There are a number of brands of pastis available, but the best known is, perhaps, Ricard.

ingredients

3 to 4 ice cubes

³/₄ measure pastis

³/₄ measure gin

³/₄ measure whisky

method

Firmly shake all of the ingredients together in a shaker and strain into a cocktail glass.

green dragon

method: shaker **glass:** large wine **ice:** cubes

These mythical beasts are popular in cocktails, and there are several green dragons, including a gin–kümmel–crème-de-menthe recipe, as well as a more recent champagne-and-Midori cocktail. This recipe may sound odd, with its inclusion of milk and cream, but you'll be pleasantly surprised by the flavour!

6 to 8 ice cubes

2 measures Pernod

2 measures milk

2 measures double cream

1 measure sugar syrup

Put 3 to 4 ice cubes in a shaker with the remaining ingredients. Shake vigorously and strain into a large, chilled, wine glass filled with the rest of the ice.

absinthe suissesse

method: shaker   **glass:** cocktail   **ice:** cubes

Absinthe and Pernod both have their origins in Switzerland, but many cocktail aficionados believe that this recipe is derived from the French speakers of Louisiana, USA. Orange-flower water is a light, non-alcoholic essence that originated in France and is used in many cocktails, notably the ramos fizz of New Orleans.

ingredients

4 to 6 ice cubes

1½ measures absinthe (or Pernod)

2–3 drops anisette

2–3 drops orange-flower water

1 tsp white crème de menthe

1 egg white

method

Place all of the ingredients in a shaker and shake vigorously. Strain into a cocktail glass.

naked waiter

method: build   **glass:** goblet   **ice:** cubes   **garnish:** lemon wedge

As its name suggests, this a modern recipe that makes great use of the anis flavour of Pernod, which was devised in Couvet, Switzerland, in 1792, by Dr Pierre Ordinaire as a 'curative' and 'restorative'. During the 1850s, in France, Pernod was prescribed to soldiers to ward off malaria!

3 to 4 ice cubes

1 measure pineapple juice

³/₄ measure Pernod

³/₄ measure Mandarine Napoleon

4 measures chilled, sparkling bitter lemon

1 lemon wedge, to garnish

Put some ice cubes into a goblet and pour in the pineapple juice, Pernod and Mandarine Napoleon. Top with the chilled bitter lemon and garnish with the wedge of lemon.

absinthe cocktail

method: mixing glass   **glass:** liqueur or cocktail   **ice:** cubes

The artist Toulouse-Lautrec not only painted the Parisian scenes that revolved around the 'green fairy', but reputedly never left home without his personal supply of absinthe contained in a long flask inside a hollowed-out walking stick. For absinthe fans, there is even a museum dedicated to it in Auvers-sur-Oise in France.

ingredients

3 to 4 ice cubes

1 $^1/_2$ measures absinthe

$^1/_2$ measure anisette

$^3/_4$ measure still mineral water

1 tsp sugar syrup

method

Put some ice cubes in a mixing glass and pour in the remaining ingredients. Stir and strain into a liqueur or cocktail glass.

If you add 1 teaspoon of maraschino to the above, you've got an 'absinthe italiano'.

pink pernod

method: build   **glass:** highball or collins   **ice:** cubes

Pernod turns milky white when mixed with water, but in this drink, it is made a perfect pink by the addition of grenadine, a cordial made from the sweetened juice of the pomegranate, *Punica granatum*.

3 to 4 ice cubes

³⁄₄ measure grenadine

³⁄₄ measure Pernod

chilled ginger ale, as required

Put some ice cubes into a highball or collins glass and pour in the grenadine and Pernod. Stir gently and top with chilled ginger ale. Stir once more.

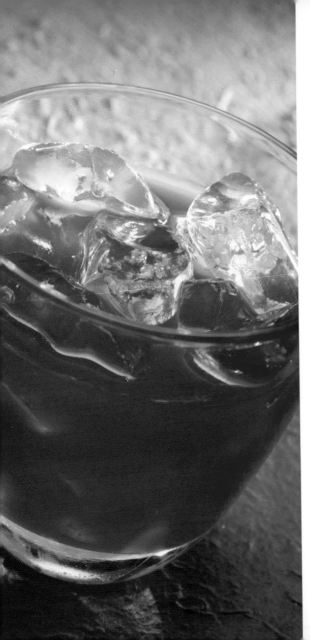

tour de france

method: build　　　　**glass:** rocks　　　　**ice:** broken

The Tour de France, as most people know, is the world's greatest cycle race. This drink appropriately uses two of France's best-loved ingredients: Pernod, whose production in France began in Pontarlier in 1805, and crème de cassis, the blackcurrant liqueur that is a speciality (along with mustard) of Dijon.

ingredients

1 scoop broken ice

1 tsp sugar syrup

1/2 measure crème de cassis

1 1/2 measures Pernod

1 measure (or more) chilled lemonade

method

Put some broken ice into a rocks glass and pour in the sugar syrup, crème de cassis and Pernod. Finally, top with the chilled lemonade.

pernod frappé

method: mixing glass   **glass:** champagne saucer   **ice:** cubes & crushed   **garnish:** maraschino cherry

A frappé is any short drink that is simply poured over crushed ice in the serving glass and served with a short straw and a cherry on a stick. Any liqueur or spirit can be used to make this refreshing drink, and frappés also make a very pleasant summer alternative to drinks that are all too often served just straight up.

2 to 3 ice cubes

2 measures Pernod

²/₃ measure anisette

1 scoop crushed ice

1 measure chilled, still mineral water

1 maraschino cherry, to garnish

Put some ice cubes in a mixing glass and pour in the Pernod and anisette. Stir and strain into a champagne saucer filled with crushed ice. Top with chilled, still mineral water to taste and garnish with a maraschino cherry on a stick.

How about a 'tiger's-eye frappé'? Use 1³/₄ measures Pernod and ½ measure peppermint schnaps.

pernod fizz

method: shaker   **glass:** highball or collins   **ice:** cubes

Fizzes are a wonderful way to enjoy a spirit or liqueur in a long, cool and refreshing drink. This Pernod-based fizz also includes a small amount of brandy and citrus juices to make a spicy, fruity mix. The drink is 'finished' with egg white to create a silvery froth.

ingredients

4 to 6 ice cubes

1 measure Pernod

2 tsps brandy

2 tsps grenadine

³/₄ measure lemon juice

³/₄ measure orange juice

1 egg white

chilled soda water, as required

method

Quarter-fill a highball or collins glass with ice. Put the remaining ingredients, except for the soda water, in a shaker. Shake well and strain into the glass. Top with soda water and stir briefly. As a final flourish, serve with a straw and a muddler.

london fog

method: shaker **glass:** cocktail **ice:** cubes **garnish:** mint sprig

The notorious London fog, known as a 'pea-souper' because it was so thick, is thankfully a thing of the past. But there is still something quite mysterious and magical about the city, even when it's shrouded in just a little light mist!

3 to 4 ice cubes

³/₄ measure anisette

³/₄ measure white crème de menthe

1 dash angostura bitters

1 mint sprig, to garnish

Place the ice cubes in a shaker and pour in the anisette, white crème de menthe and the angostura bitters. Shake and strain into a cocktail glass. Garnish with 1 mint sprig.

glad eye

method: shaker　　　　**glass:** cocktail　　　　**ice:** cubes

The word 'pastis' comes from the French *pastiche*, meaning 'a mixture'. While Ricard is probably the best-known brand, there are others available, including the 'de luxe' pastis made from no fewer than 48 herbs and spices by Henri Bardouin. In this drink, the aniseed-and-liquorice flavour of the pastis is complemented by mint.

ingredients

6 to 8 ice cubes

1 ½ measures pastis

¾ measure green crème de menthe

method

Shake the ingredients in a shaker and then strain into a cocktail glass.

anisette cocktail

The basis of this cocktail is anisette, a liqueur made from anise and aromatic herbs and spices. The sweetness of the anisette is balanced here by that old cocktail favourite, gin.

3 to 4 ice cubes

$^1/_2$ measure gin

1 measure anisette

$^1/_2$ measure whipping cream

$^1/_2$ measure egg white

grated nutmeg, to garnish

Put the ice in a shaker and pour in the gin, anisette, cream and egg white. Shake vigorously, then strain into a liqueur or cocktail glass and sprinkle a little grated nutmeg over the top.

jelly bean

method: shaker   **glass:** cocktail or shot   **ice:** cubes

This delightful mix has become popular as a shooter, but it's far too good not to linger a little longer over! Here, Pernod is combined with sloe gin – a gin in which sloes, the fruit of the blackthorn, have been macerated – and the peach- and bourbon-based liqueur, Southern Comfort.

ingredients

3 to 4 ice cubes

1 measure Pernod

1 measure sloe gin

1 measure Southern Comfort

method

Place the ice in a shaker and pour in the Pernod, sloe gin and Southern Comfort. Shake and strain into a cocktail glass (or, alternatively, into a shot glass, if you want a shooter).

all-white frappé

method: mixing glass   **glass:** large cocktail or goblet   **ice:** cubes & crushed   **garnish:** maraschino cherry

Frappés are short drinks that use almost any base spirit or liqueur and are poured over crushed ice. They are traditionally served with a short straw. This 'all-white' version combines the flavour of aniseed with chocolate and mint. A slightly sweet, herby, and very aromatic, frappé, it makes a great party or after-dinner drink.

3 to 4 ice cubes

1 measure anisette

1 measure white crème de cacao

$1/2$ measure white crème de menthe

$1/3$ measure lime juice

1 good scoop crushed ice

1 maraschino cherry, to garnish

Put the ice cubes in a mixing glass and pour in all of the remaining ingredients, except for the crushed ice and maraschino cherry. Stir well and strain into a large cocktail glass or goblet filled with crushed ice. Garnish with the maraschino cherry on a cocktail stick and serve with a short straw.

champagne cocktails

Champaigne is the Old French word for an expanse or area of open country, but to be called 'champagne', the king of wines, this sparkling wine made from Pinot and Chardonnay grapes must come from the eponymous region in northern France that is located about 160km (100 miles) north-east of Paris, and specifically from the area around Rheims and Epernay, with outposts in the Aube *département*.

Having met the first criterion of region, champagne must also be made by the *méthode champenoise*. This is the means of imparting the sparkle by secondary fermentation in each individual bottle, and not in a tank or by artificial carbonation. A vintage champagne may take eight years or more to reach maturity. There are a number of champagne types: brut, which is very dry to dry champagne; sec, which is medium-dry to sweet; demi-sec, which is sweet; and doux, which is very sweet. While each person's palate has its own preferences, in general, cocktails make use of the driest of champagnes since the recipes tend to favour the addition of sweeter liqueurs.

If it doesn't come from the Champagne region, and it is not made by the *méthode champenoise*, what you have is a 'sparkling wine'. This broad, generic term does not do real justice to the fine array of wonderful wines available: cava from Spain, sekt from Germany, spumante from Italy and cremant (also called vin mousseux), which is made in numerous wine-producing countries throughout the world. They are all made from wine through fermentation, either in tanks or using the *méthode champenoise* in bottles or by the addition of carbonic acid.

Cava (from Spain) and cremant are produced by the *méthode champenoise* of secondary fermentation in the bottle. Some fine white (and red) sparkling wines are produced from muscatel grapes, which grow only on the Crimean Peninsula, in the Ukraine. Like champagne, true Crimean sparkling wine ferments in the bottle. The labour-intensive and time-consuming process does mean that, like champagne, the sparkles persist in the glass. Asti is an important wine-growing region to the east of Turin, in the province of Piedmont, in Italy. The most famous sparkling wine is asti spumante, a sweet and fruity wine, with a low alcohol content, made from Moscato grapes.

German sekt has a minimum maturation period of nine months, and, after official testing, it is granted an official number, which must appear on the label. Prädikatssekt is a good-quality sparkling wine produced from at least 60 per cent German wine. Winzersekt is produced exclusively by the grower, or by a producer's co-operative, using the *méthode champenoise*.

While the recipes below ideally require champagne – for that is how their creators envisaged them – you can, if you wish, substitute a dry, sparkling white wine, preferably made using the *méthode champenoise* if you want those bubbles to last!

champagne charlie

The 'charlie' in this cocktail's name refers to Monsieur Charles-Camille Heidsieck, who began producing champagne in 1851. Heidsieck was a consummate salesman, as well as a celebrated *bon viveur*, which consequently earned him the nickname 'Champagne Charlie'.

1 scoop broken ice

1 measure apricot brandy

4 measures chilled champagne (preferably Charles Heidsieck)

½ slice orange, to garnish

Put some broken ice into a wine glass and pour in the apricot brandy. Add the champagne and then drop in the ½ slice of orange.

aqua marina

method: shaker   **glass:** champagne flute   **ice:** cubes

This gorgeous, sea-green cocktail gains its colour and delicate mint flavour from green crème de menthe. The addition of the vodka and lemon juice ensures that the cocktail does not become too sweet.

ingredients

3 to 4 ice cubes

1 measure vodka

1/2 measure green crème de menthe

1/2 measure lemon juice

4 measures chilled champagne

method

Shake the ingredients, except for the champagne, in a shaker and strain into a champagne flute. Top with champagne.

classic champagne cocktail

method: build   **glass:** champagne flute   **garnish:** orange slice

In 1889, a gold medal was awarded to John Dougherty, in New York, for his cocktail recipe. It turned out that Dougherty had discovered the recipe twenty-five years earlier, in the Southern states of America, but there it had a dash of spring water added. The exact origins of this cocktail classic therefore remain a mystery.

1 sugar cube

2 dashes angostura bitters

$1/3$ measure Cognac

3 measures chilled champagne

1 thin strip lemon peel

1 orange slice, to garnish

Drop the sugar cube into a champagne flute and add 2 dashes of angostura bitters, letting the sugar cube soak them up. Pour in the Cognac and then add the champagne. Squeeze the lemon peel over the top to release the oil, and then discard it. Garnish with 1 orange slice.

If you're feeling adventurous, try adding $1/3$ measure Grand Marnier and a dash of sugar syrup, too!

champagne napoleon

method: mixing glass   **glass:** champagne flute   **ice:** cubes

Legend has it that early in the morning of 18 March 1814, Napoleon Bonaparte described his battle plans to his host, the great master of champagne, Jean-Remy Moît. In recognition of Moît's achievements, Napoleon presented him with the medal of the Chevalier's Cross of the Légion d'honneur, France's highest honour. It is said that the 'medal' came from Napoleon's own uniform!

ingredients

3 to 4 ice cubes

3/4 measure Mandarine Napoleon

1 measure orange juice

3 1/4 measures chilled champagne

method

Put the ice cubes into a mixing glass and pour in the Mandarine Napoleon and the orange juice. Stir briefly, then strain into a champagne flute and, finally, add the champagne.

grand mimosa

method: build   **glass:** wine

The mimosa, an elegant mix of champagne and orange juice, was created in around 1925 at the Ritz Hotel Bar in Paris, and was named after the flower whose colour its own hue resembles. As the name suggests, this grand mimosa cocktail includes Grand Marnier.

ingredients

3 measures orange juice

1/2 measure Grand Marnier

3 measures chilled champagne

1 thin strip orange peel

method

Add the orange juice, Grand Marnier and champagne to a wine glass and twist the orange peel over the drink to release the oil before discarding it.

fiddler's toast

method: build   **glass:** goblet or large wine   **ice:** broken   **garnish:** orange slice & blue-Curaçao-soaked sugar cube

This is a fun champagne cocktail, especially with the blue sugar cube floating on its orange-slice 'raft'! The mix is distinctly fruity and sharp: lime juice, orange juice and Grand Marnier are included. If you want, capsize the 'raft' and watch the blue Curaçao leach from the sugar cube!

ingredients

1 scoop broken ice

½ measure lime juice

2 measures orange juice

⅓ measure Grand Marnier

3 measures chilled champagne

1 orange slice, to garnish

1 sugar cube soaked in blue Curaçao, to garnish

method

Put some broken ice into a goblet or large wine glass and pour in the lime juice, orange juice, Grand Marnier and champagne. Lay the orange slice on the top and float the blue-Curaçao-soaked sugar cube on it. Add a short straw.

french 75

The original 75 cocktail was a short drink created by Henry, of Henry's Bar in Paris, during World War I and named in honour of the French 75 field gun. After the war, Harry MacElhone, of Harry's Bar in Paris, added celebratory champagne and named it 'the French 75'. By 1930, the drink was so popular that had given rise to a whole range of 'French' cocktails.

ingredients

- 1 heaped tsp caster sugar
- 1 measure lemon juice
- 1 measure gin
- 4 to 6 ice cubes
- 5 measures chilled champagne
- ½ slice lemon, to garnish
- 1 cherry, to garnish

Put the caster sugar into a collins glass, pour in the lemon juice and gin and make sure that the sugar dissolves. Half-fill the glass with ice and add the champagne. Garnish with the lemon slice and cherry and serve with a straw.

Variations

French 45: use ½ tsp caster sugar and Drambuie in place of the gin.

French 65: a French 75 with 2 tsps Cognac floated on top.

French 95: 1 measure bourbon in place of the gin.

French 125: 1 measure Cognac in place of the gin.

green dragon

method: build   **glass:** champagne flute   **garnish:** green maraschino cherry

The lovely, green colour of this champagne cocktail, along with the delicate melon flavour, is courtesy of the Japanese liqueur Midori. This liqueur is a relative newcomer to the cocktail scene, but has become a very popular ingredient in modern recipes.

ingredients

1 measure Midori

4 measures chilled champagne

1 green maraschino cherry, to garnish

method

Put the Midori into a champagne flute and add the champagne. Pop the green cherry on the rim of the glass.

hotel california

method: shaker   **glass:** poco or goblet   **ice:** cubes

The American west-coast origins of this champagne cocktail are revealed in the use of tequila, made in neighbouring Mexico from the fermented and distilled juice of the agave. A very refreshing, fruit-flavoured cocktail is the result.

ingredients

6 to 8 ice cubes

2 measures pineapple juice

2 measures mandarin juice

1 measure gold tequila

4 measures chilled champagne

method

Put 2 to 3 ice cubes into a shaker and pour in the juices and the tequila. Shake and strain into a poco glass or goblet filled with the remaining ice and top with the champagne. Serve with a straw or two.

kir royale

method: build　　　　**glass:** champagne flute

The blackcurrant liqueur crème de cassis is a speciality of the Burgundy region of France. When added to white Burgundy wine, it makes a kir, which is named after Canon Kir, a wartime mayor of Dijon and left-wing politician. Here, in a truly regal version, cassis is added to the 'king of wines – champagne – to make a kir royale.

ingredients

1/3 measure crème de cassis

4 1/2 measures chilled champagne

method

Pour the crème de cassis into a champagne flute and then add the champagne.

blue splash

When blue Curaçao first became available during the 1960s, cocktail barmen (and barwomen) around the world began devising gorgeously coloured cocktails and mixed drinks that showed off its colour to real advantage. Like other Curaçaos, it has an orange flavour. This fruity, sparkling drink is great for parties; you could use sparkling white wine instead of champagne, and it would still taste wonderful!

ingredients

3 to 4 ice cubes

¾ measure gin

¾ measure blue Curaçao

¾ measure lemon juice

2 tsps dry vermouth

1 dash angostura bitters

champagne or sparkling white wine, as required

1 orange slice, to garnish

method

Put the ice cubes in a mixing glass and pour in all of the ingredients except for the champagne or sparkling white wine and the orange garnish. Strain into a rocks glass and add the champagne. Garnish with 1 orange slice.

caribbean champagne

method: build　　**glass:** champagne saucer　　**ice:** crushed　　**garnish:** banana slice

My first encounter with this cocktail was at a wonderful wedding of West Indian friends. Michael Jackson, the internationally renowned writer on drinks, quite rightly described it as being a delicious, sweet–dry extravagance. His recipe is given below, but I'm pretty certain that the one that I enjoyed contained a little more rum!

ingredients

1 scoop crushed ice

½ teaspoon white rum

½ teaspoon crème de banane

12 dashes orange bitters

4 measures chilled champagne

1 banana slice, to garnish

method

Fill a champagne saucer with crushed ice and then stir in the liquid ingredients. Garnish with the slice of banana.

palais royale

method: build   **glass:** wine   **ice:** crushed   **garnish:** ½ slice lemon & maraschino cherry

This champagne cocktail is almost a frappé, in that it is served over crushed ice. A brightly coloured cherry brandy gives it a slight pink tinge. The Dutch firms of Bols (which was founded in 1575, and is possibly the world's oldest commercial distiller) and De Kuyper, as well as the Danish company Peter Heering, all produce premium-quality cherry brandies.

ingredients

1 scoop crushed ice

1 tsp lemon juice

⅓ measure cherry brandy

1 measure Cognac

3 measures chilled champagne

½ slice lemon, to garnish

1 maraschino cherry, to garnish

method

Half-fill a wine glass with crushed ice and pour in the lemon juice, cherry brandy and Cognac. Add the champagne and garnish with a ½ lemon slice and 1 maraschino cherry.

texas fizz

Like all fizzes, this was originally made with soda water, but no doubt when the Texans struck oil, they upgraded it to champagne! Gin gives this champagne cocktail an extra kick, while the grenadine and orange juice add fruitiness and turn this long drink the colour of a Texas sunset.

ingredients

3 to 4 ice cubes

1 measure orange juice

$\frac{1}{4}$ measure grenadine

1 measure gin

1 scoop broken ice

4 measures chilled champagne

1 orange slice, to garnish

method

Put the ice cubes in a shaker and pour in the orange juice, grenadine and gin. Strain into a highball glass three-quarters filled with broken ice and add the champagne. Garnish with the slice of orange.

american glory

method: build   **glass:** highball   **ice:** cubes

Many of the classic champagne cocktails make use of fruit juices: the mimosa is simply champagne and orange juice, while a buck's fizz has a splash of grenadine added. This orange-flavoured cocktail uses orange juice and lemonade to give it an extra sparkle.

ingredients

3 to 4 ice cubes

2 measures orange juice

2 measures chilled lemonade

3 measures chilled champagne

method

Put the ice cubes in a highball glass and pour in the orange juice and lemonade. Finally, add the champagne.

mango bellini

method: build   **glass:** champagne flute   **garnish:** peach slice & cherry

One of the most famous champagne cocktails, the bellini was created by Giuseppi Cipriani in 1943, at Harry's Bar, Venice, to celebrate the exhibition of the Venetian artist Bellini. The classic version used peach juice, whereas this contemporary version uses mango juice.

ingredients

1½ measures mango juice

1 tsp sugar syrup

3 measures chilled champagne

1 peach slice

1 cherry

method

Mix together the mango juice and the sugar syrup and pour into a champagne flute. Pour in the champagne and garnish with a slice of peach and a cherry.

andalusia

method: build   **glass:** champagne flute   **garnish:** maraschino cherry

Jerez (which was far too difficult for the English to pronounce with the proper 'lisp', and so became became 'sherry'!) is the capital of the sherry-producing region that runs between Cadiz and Seville, in Spain's most southerly region, namely Andalusia.

ingredients

1 measure sweet sherry

3 measures chilled champagne

1 maraschino cherry, to garnish

method

Pour the sherry into a champagne flute and add the champagne. Perch the cherry on the rim of the glass.

shooters and shots

In the old Hollywood Western movies, cowboys and outlaws swung by the saloon and downed a shot of whiskey or two fingers (two ounces) in one swallow. Since then, shots or shooters, tooters and slammers have been made with a huge range of wonderful spirits and mixers in bright, colourful concoctions with the most outrageous names and decorated with miniature garnishes.

Shooters not only taste good, they can also be made up in large batches rather than in individual servings, saving you time to enjoy them with friends at a party or celebration. Popular in many bars, bartenders have gone to great lengths to develop exciting new flavours in shooters as well as themed drinks for special occasions. You can serve shooters in shot glasses and there is a huge range of styles available, including novelty shots in the shape of cowboy boots or wild animals. You can even get your own shot glass attached to a necklace! Tooters are a new departure: in some bars these are served in glasses that look remarkably like laboratory test tubes and are held in a rack, while in some kitsch Western-themed bars, staff carry tooters in holsters that look a little like the gun belts worn by cowboys in the movies, but in place of bullets are the tooter tubes.

Frequently the spirit, or lower-proof liqueur, is also combined with one or more juices and the small size of the drinks themselves limits the amount of alcohol contained in each drink. However, in some cases, shooters can be pretty hard stuff! You will find a range of recipes in this book to suit both preferences.

Some of the drinks on offer in this book are technically known among bartenders as pousse-cafés or after-coffees. A pousse-café is more a style of presentation than a class of drink, as there are no common components, although drinks have been served in this style for centuries. Served after dinner, these cocktails consist of several liqueurs or spirits of specific gravities that sit in layers in the glass. The liqueur layers should strictly remain separated, one above the other, although it does take practice and a steady hand to get them absolutely perfect! Each liquor has a different density: basically syrups are heavier than liqueurs, and spirits are lighter. You will need to pour the heaviest density into the glass first, then the next lightest is poured carefully and slowly over the back of a spoon so that it settles in a separate layer, then the next lightest liquor is added.

Pousse-cafés usually have at least three layers, but there are some beautiful and delicious drinks to be made with just two layers: it's worth practising with these first to perfect your technique. Pousse-cafés are traditionally served in their own glass: a small, straight-sided, short-stemmed, tube-shaped glass. You could also use a parfait glass or even a cordial glass, sometimes called a pony, which looks like a small white wine glass, but the top has a narrower opening than the base of the bowl. Some well-known pousse-cafés like the B-52 can also be served stirred, strained and on the rocks, and you will find suggestions for alternative ways of serving.

Shooters provide a perfect opportunity to be experimental. First, to try out those strange liquors in often very fancy bottles, and secondly, to adapt recipes to suit your own taste. After all, that's how many cocktails, mixed drinks and shooters were devised! The great fun with shooters, and especially jelly shots, is that it gives you an opportunity to break out that interesting looking bottle of stuff you got on holiday! You'll have so much fun that you'll be searching out more and more exotic ingredients for future use!

To get you familiar with shooters, this book is divided into four sections. In the first chapter, Shots in the Dark, you'll find recipes for shots that don't require any skills beyond pouring liquors into a glass! They're so easy to make, you could (almost!) make them blindfolded!

The second chapter, Shaky Shots, is all about shooters made in a cocktail shaker. These shaky shots are also very easy to make, but instead of pouring into a glass, you pour the liquors into a shaker with ice, shake, and then strain the chilled liquor into the shot glass. Shaking with ice is one way of blending the ingredients into a smooth mix. It also increases the volume of the drink because a little water from the melted ice will find its way into each glass. Shaky shots are fun to make and using a shaker allows you to make up a batch of shooters to fill six shot glasses.

In Trick Shots you'll find recipes for 2- and 3-layered shooters, so you can practice your steady hand skills and impress your party guests! You can have great fun with flavour and colour combinations with these shooters, and making them can be a party game in itself! And, if they don't turn out to be perfect examples of pousse-cafés, it doesn't matter, because you can always mix them up and they'll taste just as good!

You'll find some recipes for party shooters in the Six Shooters chapter, and in this section there are also some recipes for the latest trend in shooters: gelatine shots. Pretty well any cocktail or shooter recipe can be adapted into a jiggelo or jelly shot. You can eat them by squeezing them out of their plastic shot glass, or, if you have set them in glass shots, eat them with a spoon! And if you don't have enough glasses to go round, you can always set the jelly in a shallow dish or tray and cut out jelly shapes with cookie cutters! With jelly shots, you get shots without losing a drop!

If you're throwing a party and are serving shots, there are a few things to remember:

• Shooters generally contain 5.7 cl/2 fl oz of alcoholic mix. A glance at the recipes will tell you which ones are softer because of the addition of fruit juices and mixers, and which ones are harder as they contain more alcohol per shot. Consequently, three shooters per person, four maximum, will be enough to satisfy!

• Shooters are drinks designed to be downed in one, but you may like a drink so much you want to sip it. That's perfectly all right. For those who down in one, make sure there are plenty of glasses of water and fruit juices available as chasers.

• Responsible drinking is the key to enjoyment, health, and safety, both personally, and the safety of others, especially if you are a driver. Do not drink and drive, and never offer 'one for the road'.

• Do not condone or encourage underage drinking: The recipes in this book are intended for adults. There are numerous non-alcoholic fruity syrups that can be used to create delicious blank bullets or mock shots. You will find that these are very popular with many people because they are so tasty. So, be prepared when you entertain to provide them for all your guests!

• Do not push an alcoholic drink onto a guest: if they say no, they mean no. Offer delicious juices and sparkling minerals instead.

• Never, ever, spike anyone's drink: they may be the designated driver that night; be allergic to alcohol; be on medication; have religious beliefs which preclude alcohol, or they may be in recovery.

Shots in the Dark
Quick Shots & Slammers

In this section, all the recipes are very simple to make. In most cases you just have to pour the ingredients into a shot glass, although one or two do make use of really chilled ingredients. In these instances, you can refrigerate the ingredients well in advance, or if you need to chill them down in a hurry, stir or shake them with ice cubes, and then strain the liquor into the glass.

Although the glasses may seem small, a shot glass is about 5.7 cl/ 2 fl oz, so they are nevertheless packed full of alcohol, and two or three shots per person should be plenty! Make sure you have plenty of water, juices and maybe a few beers as well for chasers!

There are plenty of opportunities to try your favourite tipple as well as some interesting liqueurs and spirit combinations in shots. Take a look at the recipes and choose your weapon!

Gin & Beer It

1 part gin • 1 part beer

The pun may be awful, but the drink is very tasty indeed: gin is one of the most popular spirits in cocktails and mixed drinks.

method

Don't pre-chill the gin or beer, just pour them straight -into the shot glass.

Amaretto Slammer

1 part Amaretto • 1 Splash of lemon-lime soda

A nice introduction to slammers! The trick is to drink the shot before it fizzes over the glass! Amaretto has a delicate almond flavour which is given a little sharpness here by the lemon-lime soda.

method

Put the Amaretto into the shot glass and add the splash of lemon-lime soda. Place a napkin, or clean hand, over the glass. Raise the glass 2 or 3 inches, then rap firmly on the bar or table. Drink quickly while it's still fizzing.

For the classic Tequila Slammer just replace the Amaretto with tequila.

Astronaut Shooter

1 part chilled vodka • 1 lemon wedge • Sugar
Instant coffee powder

You might not expect to find instant coffee in a shooter, but this combination is truly out of this world. Too many, and you'll surely be seeing stars.

method

Coat the lemon wedge on one side with sugar and the other with the powdered instant coffee. Really chill the vodka, shake, not stir it, with some ice, then strain into the shot glass. Suck the lemon and then shoot the vodka.

Don Quixote

1 part Guinness stout • 1 part tequila

In honour of Cervantes' hero, but why not make
two: one for Don Quixote and one for his trusty
sidekick, Sancho Panza. A couple of these and you'll
soon be tilting at windmills too!

method

Don't pre-chill the ingredients, just pour into a shot
glass.

Fire Truck

1 part Jagermeister • 1 part ginger ale

A fiery combination that may have you calling the emergency services! Jagermeister is a German 'bitters' with a rich, herby flavour. The name means 'master of the hunt'.

method

Chill the Jagermeister. You can shake or stir it with ice first, then strain into a shot glass. Then pour in the ginger ale. To make a Firetruck with a Siren, add 1 part vodka.

Lemon Drop

1 part spice rum (or citrus vodka) • 1 lemon wedge
1 teaspoon sugar

You may well remember the bittersweet lemon drop
sweets you could get as a kid. This is the grown-up
version. Which taste nicer? Suck 'em and see!

method

Place the sugar on the lemon, shoot the rum
(or vodka) and the suck the lemon.

An alternative, and only for close friends, is called a
Body Shot: 1 part vodka; 1 individual packet of
sugar; 1 lemon wedge. Pour the sugar onto your
friend's neck. Put the lemon wedge skin-side inwards
into their mouth. First you lick their sugared neck,
then shoot the vodka and finally suck the lemon
from their mouth!

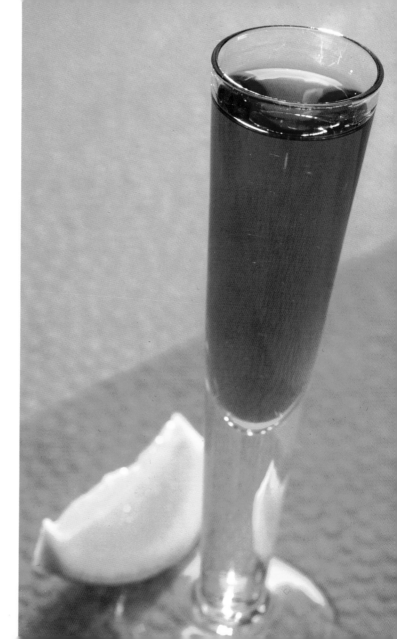

Cordless Screwdriver

1 part vodka • 1 orange wedge • 1 teaspoon sugar

The original long screwdriver appeared in the 1950s and evidently got its name from a US oil man in Iran who stirred his drink with one of his screwdrivers. Try this cordless version!

method

Chill the vodka. You could shake or stir it with ice and then strain into the shot glass. Dip the orange wedge into the sugar. Shoot the vodka and then immediately suck the orange wedge.

For a Rum Screw, replace the vodka with white rum. For a Super Screw use 1 part vodka, 1 part orange juice and 1 part soda water. Pour into a glass neat.

Dr Pepper

1 shot glass Amaretto • 1 glass of beer

Can't manage a whole beer? Try this half-size version then! This drink tastes just like pop, but has more of a kick. Why not try a flaming Dr Pepper? Just add a drop of rum and ignite before dropping the shot into the beer – but take care!

method

Drop the shot glass of Amaretto into the beer and drink before it foams over!

Boiler Maker

One 12-ounce/350ml beer • 1 shot glass of whisk(e)y

This is a classic, but make sure you don't break your teeth on the shot glass! This drink originated in the 1920s, when it was a favourite with big, strong working men!

method

Fill a glass with 12 ounces/350ml of beer and a shot glass with whisk(e)y of your choice. Hold the shot glass of whisk(e)y over the beer and gently drop it in.

For a variation on the Boiler Maker, try a Depth Charge using 1 shot glass of peppermint schnapps.

Dakota

1 part bourbon • 1 part tequila

Two states united in one! An unusual combination
of Bourbon whiskey and Mexico's national spirit,
tequila, but one that will have you coming back
for more.

method

Don't pre-chill the ingredients, just pour them into
a shot glass and shoot.

Southern Pepper Slammer

I part Southern Comfort • I part Dr Pepper soda

A delicious, fizzy combination of sweet peach and spicy Dr Pepper. Packs quite a wallop!

method

Don't chill the ingredients, just pour the Southern Comfort into the shot glass and add the Dr Pepper.
For
a So Co Slammer, use 1 part cola in place of the Dr Pepper.

Dead Bird

1 part Jagermeister • 1 part Wild Turkey

A chance to use Germany's famous bitter, Jagermeister, whose name means 'master of the hunt'. That's why this Wild Turkey, a straight Kentucky bourbon, is a dead bird!

method

Don't chill the ingredients, just pour into the shot glass. Take aim and shoot!

Funky Chicken

I part Wild Turkey • I part tequila

Another bird, another good reason to get the Wild Turkey out! This one will have you dancing around the room!

method

Simply pour the ingredients into the shot glass neat. Don't chill them first. Shoot!

Brain Eraser

1 part vodka • 1 part Amaretto • 1 part coffee liqueur
(Tia Maria or Kahlua) • Dash of soda

This shooter you drink through a straw all at
once! You'll almost be able to feel those brain
cells floating away.

method

Fill a glass with crushed ice and add the vodka,
Amaretto and coffee liqueur. Top with a dash of
soda and drink it down all in one go through a
straw.

Bandera

1 part lime juice • 1 part tequila • 1 part tomato juice

The word *bandera* is Spanish for 'flag', and the flag in question here is the Mexican flag. A perfect way to celebrate the country's national day on 1st May.

method

Take 3 shot glasses and line them up in front of you. Fill the first glass with lime juice, the second glass with tequila and the third with tomato juice: you now have the three parts of the Mexican flag! Start with the lime juice and shoot them all as fast as you can in that order!

Black Rain

1 part Sambuca Negra (Black Sambuca)
3 parts chilled champagne

A very smart shot, like a pearl-handled revolver!
Black Sambuca has a licquorice-aniseed flavour with
just a hint of coffee.

method

Pour the Sambuca Negra into the shot glass and
add the chilled champagne.

Manchurian Candidate

1 part chilled vodka • 1 part soy sauce

Watch the movie, catch the remake, try the shot!
Just make sure you don't have too many, as you may
find someone trying to brainwash you!

method

Chill the vodka – you can either shake or stir it
with ice cubes, then strain into the shot glass. Add
the soy sauce. For a Black Samurai, substitute the
vodka with 2 parts sake! Kampai!

T.N.T.

I part tequila • I part tonic water

The combination sounds gentle enough: after all, what could be explosive about tonic water? But mixed with tequila, it's pure dynamite!

method

Don't pre-chill the tequila or tonic water. Pour them straight up into the shot glass.

Blood Clot

1 part Southern Comfort • Splash of Grenadine

A gruesome name, but it has to be said, this is exactly what it looks like! Don't let the name put you off – it's a very tasty shot!

method

Don't chill the ingredients, just pour the Southern Comfort into the shot glass and add the splash of Grenadine to make the blood clot!

Tablazo

I part ginger ale • I part vodka

What does the name mean? We don't know, but it sounds like a fiery drink, and indeed it is. Put your hand over the glass, slam it on a table and drink it before you lose it!

method

Pour the ingredients straight into a shot glass.

Klondike

1 part Baileys Irish Cream • 1 part Jagermeister

You'll certainly get a rush from this drink. And while it might not make you rich, you'll have a golden glow! Just don't drink too many. You know what they say about fool's gold, and no one wants to be a fool, do they?

method

Pour the ingredients neat into the shot glass.

Orange Crush Shooter

1 part vodka • 1 part Triple Sec/Cointreau
1 part soda water

Orange Crush is a nice, fruity soft drink, perfect for a summer's day. This shooter is a nice fruit drink with a kick! Still perfect for summer though, day or night!

method

Don't pre-chill the ingredients. Pour the vodka and Triple Sec/Cointreau into the shot glass and add the soda.

Jack Hammer

I part Jack Daniels • I part tequila

If you're wondering how this drink got its name, try a couple of them. There, can you feel the pounding in your head? What does it remind you of? Exactly!

method

Pour the Jack Daniels and tequila straight into a shot glass.

Burning Cherry

1 part bourbon • 1 part whiskey • 1 part Scotch
Dash of Grenadine

If whisk(e)y is your poison, this is for you! With 3 different varieties combined, this should probably be called a Smokin' Cherry.

method

Don't pre-chill the ingredients. Pour the whiskies into a shot glass neat and top with the dash of Grenadine. Give a quick stir before slamming.

CHPOK

1 part chilled vodka • 2 parts chilled champagne

Not a misprint put a delicious combination of champagne and vodka. Don't make the mistake of serving this at a wedding reception however. Not unless you want the guests CHPOK-ing all over the place.

method

Get the ingredients really cold beforehand and then pour the vodka into the glass and add the champagne.

Italian Russian

1 part vodka • 1 part Sambuca

Could be an Italov or a Russital. The chill of the vodka, mixed with the heat of the Sambuca will make everyone seem like a comrade.

method

Pour the ingredients straight into a shot glass. Don't pre-chill the ingredients.

Dirty Rotten Scoundrel

1 part vodka • 1 part melon liqueur

Bad day at the office? Boss getting you down? Forget it all with one of these! The satisfaction you'll get from pounding this shot on the table will relieve all your frustrations.

method

Don't chill the vodka or melon liqueur, just pour into a shot glass.

Malibu Cola

I part Malibu • I part cola

How easy can a shot be? Fruit and fizz make a delicious combination, and the glow you'll get will make you feel as if you're basking in the Malibu sunshine.

method

Don't pre-chill the ingredients, just pour the Malibu into the shot glass and add the cola.

Horny Bull

No.1: 1 part tequila • 1 part Southern Comfort
No.2: 1 part tequila • 1 part rum • 1 part vodka
No.3: 1 part tequila • 1 part light rum

There are a couple of variations: try them all out for size! The photograph shows a no. 1. Just keep away from red rags and you'll be fine.

method

Don't pre-chill the ingredients, simply pour the ingredients into the shot glass. Grab the bull by the horns and shoot!

Horny Mohican

1 part crème de banane • 1 part Baileys Irish Cream
1 part coconut rum

This drink has so much bite it will make your hair stand on end! Perfect for old-school punks and rockers. The creamy taste is very misleading: a few of these and you'll be pogo-ing till dawn.

method

Don't pre-chill the ingredients, just pour them into the shot glass.

Fancy a Horny Girl Scout? 1 part coffee liqueur and 1 part peppermint schnapps poured straight into a shot glass. Be prepared!

Jageritia

I part Jagermeister • I part tequila • I part lime juice

If you want something a little more ferocious than a cocktail, try this Margarita with attitude. You'll be dancing around your sombrero all night.

method

Don't chill the ingredients, just pour them straight into the shot glass.

Joe Cocker

1 part Amaretto • 1 part Southern Comfort
1 part Crown Royal bourbon • 1 part whiskey

Get by with a little help from this little friend. The original recipe called for Crown Royal bourbon, but Joe's a nice guy so he won't mind if you substitute!

method

Pour the ingredients straight – don't pre-chill into a shot glass. Now you know where Joe Cocker gets that magnificent scream!

Three Wise Men

1 part whisk(e)y • 1 part Jim Beam bourbon
1 part tequila

Wise men are like buses, you wait for ages, then three come along! We make no claim that this drink will make you any wiser, however.

method

Don't chill the ingredients, just pour straight into the shot glass.

How about Three Wise Men on a Farm? 1 part whisk(e)y; 1 part Jim Beam; 1 part Wild Turkey; 1 part Yukon Jack (a sweet, Canadian herb liqueur).

Meat & Potatoes

1 part vodka • 1 slice pepperoni

A fun shot for parties, and a lot quicker than preparing a Sunday roast! Make sure you use potato-based vodka, as meat and fruit doesn't have the same ring to it.

method

Chill the vodka – you can shake or stir with ice – and then strain into a shot glass. Garnish with the slice of pepperoni. It's a meal in a glass!

M & M

1 part Frangelico • 1 part white crème de cacao

Oooh, this one's for chocoholics everywhere. What could be more perfect than combining two vices at once: chocolate and alcohol? Pure decadence in a glass.

method

Don't chill the ingredients beforehand, just pour them straight into the shot glass.

Alien

1 part blue curacao • Splash of Baileys Irish Cream

The colour is like something from another planet, and the taste is out of this world. An alien invasion has never felt so good.

method

Chill the blue curacao – you can stir or shake it first with ice in the shaker to get it really cold – then strain into the shot glass. Slowly pour the Baileys into the centre and watch the alien life form appear.

Baby Guinness

1 part coffee liqueur (Tia Maria or Kahlua)
Splash of Baileys Irish Cream

It looks like a tiny glass of Guinness, it tastes like nectar. Try mixing up a batch for a special party, and you'll be singing Danny Boy like a good 'un.

method

Pour the coffee liqueur into the shot glass. Now, very slowly, pour the Baileys over the back (the rounded side) of a spoon to float on top. If you prefer, you could use a turkey baster to float the Baileys!

Clear Layer Shot

*I part lemon-lime soda • I part akvavit
I part Grenadine*

A fun shot – with luck, the akvavit should settle in a layer at the top of the glass, but don't worry if it doesn't because the flavour combination is terrific however it works out.

method

Combine the akvavit and the lemon-lime soda in the glass. Slowly pour the Grenadine down the inside of the glass. It should settle into a layer at the bottom.

Cement Mixer

I part Baileys Irish Cream • I part sweetened lime juice

Because Baileys Irish Cream (unlike crème liqueurs) does contain cream, mixing it with citrus juices will make it curdle. Most of the time in cocktails and mixed drinks this is avoided, but in shots, it makes for a very interesting experience!

method

Pour the Baileys into the shot glass and carefully pour the sweetened lime juice over the back (the rounded side) of a spoon so it floats on top. (If you want, you can use a turkey baster to add the lime juice!) The lime juice will cause the Baileys to curdle. Take the shot but roll it around in your mouth before swallowing!

Shaky Shots

These shots are made using a cocktail shaker. Simply put some ice cubes in the bottom of the shaker, pour in the ingredients, put the top on, and shake! The liquor is strained through the holes, leaving the ice behind. This makes the ingredients really chilled and thoroughly mixed together, but it does increase the volume of the drinks as you will be adding a little iced water each time. Make sure you measure accurately – use those graduated kitchen measuring spoons – and take account of the extra volume as you don't want to waste any of your precious shots!

Where a recipe includes a fizzy soda or mixer, I find it best to add this to the mix after shaking the other ingredients together and giving the whole mix a stir with a long-handled spoon or muddler. Shaking a fizzy ingredient in the shaker risks a foaming mass when you undo the cap – especially if you are making up a large batch of a recipe.

If you don't have a shaker, don't worry. You can always stir the ingredients really well together in a jug with ice cubes, then strain through a fine mesh sieve to keep the ice back.

Some of these shots were created using proprietary (branded) spirits and liqueurs and this is often reflected in their names. The original recipes are given, and while it's quite possible to substitute a proprietary spirit or liqueur with a generic version, bear in mind that any substitution will affect the final taste.

Some of the recipes call for what is known as sweet and sour mix: this is a blend of half and egg white; 85g/3oz sugar; 250ml/9fl oz lemon juice and 250ml/9fl oz water.

Acapulco

1 part tequila • 1 part pineapple juice
1 part grapefruit juice

A touch of Mexican sunshine brought to you in a mix of tequila, pineapple and grapefruit juice..

method

Put some ice cubes into the shaker and pour in the juices. Add the tequila. Shake well and strain into a shot glass.

Absolut Quaalude

1 part Absolut vodka • 1 part Frangelico
1 part Baileys Irish Cream

An equally addictive alternative! Like the Hunter, also from the makers of Absolut Vodka, it makes use of coffee and hazelnut flavours.

method

Put some ice cubes into the shaker and pour in the ingredients. Shake well and strain into a shot glass.

Absolut Testa Rossa

2 parts Absolut vodka • 1 part Campari

Absolut vodka is here combined with Campari, the famous red-coloured Italian 'bitters', hence the 'Festa Rossa' (red head) name.

method

Place the ingredients in the shaker with some ice cubes. Shake and then strain into a shot glass.

Absolut Hunter

2 parts Absolut vodka • 1 part Jagermeister

This recipe comes courtesy of the makers of
Absolut Vodka, which is mixed here with
Jagermeister, a herby German 'bitters'.

method

Put some ice cubes in the shaker and pour in the
Absolut vodka and Jagermeister. Shake and strain
into
a shot glass.

Advo Shot

2 parts blue curacao • 1 part Advocaat

Advocaat is a brandy-and-egg liqueur that is a speciality of Holland. Try this blue-orange mix!

method

Shake the ingredients with ice cubes in the shaker then strain into a shot glass.

American Apple Pie

1 part cinnamon schnapps • 1 part apple juice

Apple pie with cinnamon in a glass! Cinnamon schnapps is just one of the numerous flavours available, and is terrific with apple juice.

method

Shake the ingredients with ice and then strain into a shot glass.

Coma

1 part dark rum • 1 part cinnamon schnapps

There are a few shots called Coma, testament to the effects of one too many! This version is an opportunity to use cinnamon schnapps.

method

Shake the ingredients with ice then strain into a shot glass.

After Dinner

Perfect for, well, after dinner! This is one shot you may prefer to 'sip' rather than 'shoot' – it tastes so good you won't want it to end!

method

Put the ingredients into a shaker along with some ice cubes. Shake and strain into a shot glass.

All Fall Down

1 part tequila • 1 part Kahlua • 1 part dark rum

That's what will happen after a couple of these shots! Rum and tequila are combined with coffee-flavoured Kahlua, a speciality of Mexico.

method

Put some ice cubes into a shaker and pour in the ingredients. Shake well and strain into a shot glass.

Alabama Slammer

No.1: 1 part Southern Comfort • 1 part Amaretto
Splash orange juice • Splash pineapple juice

No2: 2 parts Southern Comfort • 2 parts Amaretto
1 part sloe gin • Splash lemon juice

No3: 2 parts Southern Comfort • 1 part Amaretto
4 parts cranberry juice

There are a couple of variations on this theme – try them out for yourself. The photograph shows No. 1.

method

Put the ingredients into a shaker along with some ice cubes. Shake and strain into a shot glass.

Alice from Dallas Shooter

1 part coffee liqueur (Tia Maria or Kahlua)
1 part Mandarine Napoleon • 1 part tequila gold

Beware those Texas gals! The smooth taste of this shot disguises a drink that packs a pretty powerful punch!

method

Put some ice cubes into a shaker and pour in the ingredients. Shake well and strain into a shot glass.

Agent Orange

A glorious colour and a taste to match. This shot makes use of two of America's finest products: the delicate peach-flavoured Suuthern Comfort and the famous Tennessee sour mash whiskey from Jack Daniels.

method

Shake the ingredients with ice cubes then strain into a shot glass.

Alternate

1 part crème de cassis • 1 part Midori
1 part pineapple juice

A pleasant change. Cassis is a crème liqueur made
from blackcurrants, a speciality of Dijon in France,
while Midori is the bright green, melon-flavoured
liqueur from Japan.

method

Pour the ingredients into the shaker, along with
some ice cubes. Shake and then strain into a shot
glass.

Amalfi Drive

I part crème de banane • I part limoncello

Lemon trees line the streets of towns like Amalfi on the Bay of Naples in Italy. This shot uses limoncello, an intensely lemon-flavoured liqueur.

method

Put some ice cubes into a shaker and pour in the ingredients. Shake well and strain into a shot glass.

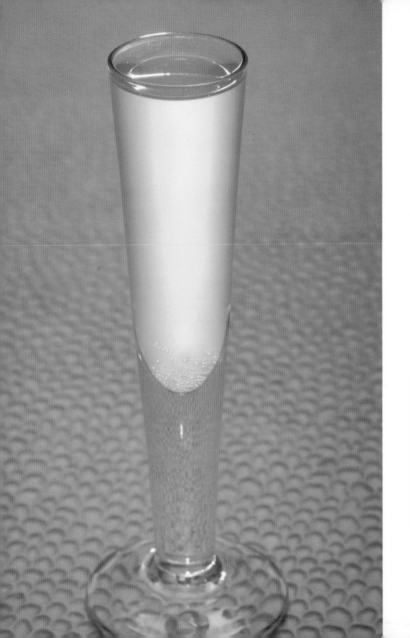

Amaretto Chill

1 part vodka • 1 part Amaretto
1 part pineapple juice • 1 part lemonade

A fruity-almond flavoured shot, based on vodka and Amaretto, the deep amber-coloured, Italian liqueur.

method

Put some ice cubes into the shaker and pour in the pineapple juice, the vodka and the Amaretto. Shake well. Take the lid off the shaker and pour in the lemonade. Stir. Put the cap back on the shaker and strain the drink into a shot glass.

Amaretto Kamikaze

1 part vodka • 1 part Amaretto

Kamikaze means 'divine wind'. This shot is a breeze! But beware: 2 or 3 could produce devastating effects!

method

Put some ice cubes into a shaker and pour in the ingredients. Shake well and strain into a shot glass. For an Amaretto Kumihuzi, replace the vodka with tequila.

Angels Rush Shooter

1 part Frangelico • 1 part cream

A creamy concoction with the flavour of hazelnuts. Made for angels, but available to mortals too!

method

Put some ice cubes in the shaker and pour in the cream and Frangelico. Shake well and strain into a shot glass. Listen for the sound of angels' harps!

American Dream

1 part coffee liqueur (Tia Maria or Kahlúa)
1 part Amaretto • 1 part Frangelico
1 part dark crème de cacao

Live the dream! This shot combines the flavour of nuts – almonds and hazelnuts – with chocolate and coffee.

method

Put the ingredients in the shaker along with some ice cubes and shake. Strain into a shot glass

Angry Fijian

1 part crème de banane • 1 part Malibu

Can't imagine why anyone could be angry after this coconut banana delight!

method

Put some ice cubes into a shaker and pour in the ingredients. Shake well and strain into a shot glass.

Electric Kamikaze

1 part vodka • 1 part Triple Sec/Cointreau
1 part blue curacao • 1 part lime juice

Watch the sparks fly! The gorgeous colour in the shot is provided by the blue curacao, which has a distinct orange flavour.

method

Put the ingredients in the shaker along with some ice cubes and shake. Strain into a shot glass.

Antifreeze

1 part vodka • 1 part green crème de menthe

Perfect for raising the temperature a few degrees!
The colour and the mint flavour come from the
green crème de menthe.

method

Put some ice cubes into a shaker and pour in the
ingredients. Shake well and strain into a shot glass.

Apricot Chill

A fire and ice mix, courtesy of the apricot brandy.
Not a 'true' brandy, apricot brandy is made by
infusing the fruit in a spirit base.

method

Put some ice cubes into a shaker and pour in the
ingredients. Shake well and strain into a shot glass.

Bootlegger

1 part whisk(e)y • 1 part Southern Comfort
1 part Sambuca

Respect to all those prohibition-busters! Whiskey, peach-flavoured Southern Comfort and a hint of licquorice makes a very smooth shot.

method

Put some ice cubes into a shaker and pour in the ingredients. Shake well and strain into a shot glass.

B-54

1 part Baileys Irish Cream • 1 part Tia Maria or Kahlua coffee liqueur • 1 part green crème de menthe • 1 part Grand Marnier

Some say this has more fire power than a B-52! it's certainly an interesting combination of flavours.

method

Put the ingredients in the shaker along with some ice cubes and shake well. Strain into a shot glass.

Backstreet Romeo

1 part whiskey – preferably Irish!
1 part Baileys Irish Cream

Girls, this is the boy your mum warned you about!
The smoothness of the creamy Baileys hides the
knock-out effect of the whiskey!

method

Put the ingredients in the shaker along with some
ice cubes and shake well. Strain into a shot glass.

Ballistic Missile

1 part Grand Marnier • 1 part Amaretto
1 part pineapple juice

Does what it says on the label. A cognac-based
liqueur, Grand Marnier is the 'king' of the curacaos.

method

Put some ice cubes into a shaker and pour in the
ingredients. Shake well and strain into a shot glass.

Bananarama

1 part vodka • 1 part crème de banane

Remember them? Remember the songs? If you can, you're old enough to be drinking this!

method

Put the ingredients in the shaker along with some ice cubes and shake. Strain into a shot glass.

Cactus Thorn

2 parts silver tequila • 1 part green crème de menthe
1 part freshly squeezed mint juice

Watch out, they're sharp! The 'cactus' refers to
the tequila, and the green colour comes from the
crème de menthe.

method

Put the ingredients in the shaker along with some
ice cubes and shake. Strain into a shot glass.

Black Forest Gateau

1 part cherry brandy • 1 part Tia Maria or Kahlua coffee liqueur • 1 part Baileys Irish Cream

Liquid cake! Cherry liqueur combined with a hint of coffee and lashings of cream.

method

Put the ingredients in the shaker along with some ice cubes and shake. Strain into a shot glass.

Blue Marlin

2 parts light rum • 1 part blue curacao
1 part lime juice

One big fish that didn't get away! The sweetness of
the orange-flavoured blue curacao is tempered by
the rum and lime juice.

method

Put the ingredients in the shaker along with some
ice cubes and shake. Strain into a shot glass.

Avalanche

*1 part Southern Comfort • 1 part coffee liqueur
(Tia Maria or Kahlua) • 1 part dark crème de cacao*

Starts slow, then builds in strength until it knocks
you over!

method

Put some ice cubes into a shaker and pour in the
ingredients. Shake well and strain into a shot glass.

Broken Down Golf Cart

1 part Amaretto • 1 part Midori • 1 part cranberry juice

Fortunately, it broke down on the 18th close to the clubhouse, where this remarkable mix gets things back on par.

method

Put some ice cubes into a shaker and pour in the ingredients. Shake well and strain into a shot glass.

Bat Bite

1 part Bacardi rum • 1 part cranberry juice

This drink comes from the bat logo of the world-famous Bacardi rum. Bats lived in the caves where the rum was aged!

method

Put some ice cubes into a shaker and pour in the ingredients. Shake well and strain into a shot glass.

California Surfer

1 part Malibu • 1 part Jagermeister
2 parts pineapple juice

Surfs up! A delicious combination of coconut
rum and Jagermeister!

method

Put the ingredients in the shaker along with some
ice cubes and shake. Strain into a shot glass.

Cream of Beef

I part Baileys Irish Cream • I part Beefeater gin

The cream is Baileys, the beef is Beefeater gin, of course!

method

Put the ingredients in the shaker along with some ice cubes and shake. Strain into a shot glass.

Catfish

3 parts bourbon • 1 part peach schnapps

There's a sign on my door that says: Gone fishing!
There's a fair amount of bourbon in here and an
extra kick from the peach schnapps.

method

Put some ice cubes into a shaker and pour in the
ingredients. Shake well and strain into a shot glass.

Champerelle

1 part anisette • 1 part cognac • 1 part Cointreau

Ooh-la-la! France's finest produce in a neat little hsot with an aniseed flavour.

method

Put the ingredients in the shaker along with some ice cubes and shake. Strain into a shot glass.

Choad

1 part green Chartreuse • 1 part tequila

Weird but wonderful! Green Chartreuse has been made since the 16th century by monks in France, while tequila was the tipple of the Aztec gods of Mexico.

method

Put the ingredients in the shaker along with some ice cubes and shake. Strain into a shot glass.

Comfort Special

2 parts Southern Comfort • 1 part sweet vermouth
1 part orange juice

Just peachy! Southern Comfort was 'invented' by W. Heron in New Orleans in the 1880s. When he moved to St Louis he created the St Louis Cocktail, made with his secret-recipe peach-flavoured liqueur.

method

Put some ice cubes into a shaker and pour in the ingredients. Shake well and strain into a shot glass.

Calypso Cooler

1 part spiced rum • 1 part Amaretto
1 part orange juice • Dash of Grenadine

One for drinking aboard Jacques Cousteau's boat!
Spiced rum gives this shot an interesting 'bite':
try Captain Morgan's, one of the finest
proprietary brands. —

method

Pour the spiced rum, Amaretto and orange juice
into the shaker along with some ice cubes and
shake. Strain into a shot glass and top with the dash
of Grenadine.

Cuervo Aztec Sky

1 part José Cuervo tequila • 1 part blue curacao

A tequila and blue curacao mix courtesy of José Cuervo tequila.

method

Put some ice cubes into a shaker and pour in the ingredients. Shake well and strain into a shot glass.

For a Cuervo Aztec Ruin replace the blue curacao with Roses Lime Juice.

Deckchair

1 part Southern Comfort • 1 part crème de banane
1 part orange juice

Relaxez-vous with this fruity delight – a delicious
mix of peach, banana and orange flavours.

method

Put some ice cubes into a shaker and pour in the
ingredients. Shake well and strain into a shot glass.

Death from Within

1 part light rum • 1 part dark rum • 1 part vodka

A potent little minx! Feel the heat rise up inside
after you've downed this shot!

method

Put the ingredients in the shaker along with some
ice cubes and shake. Strain into a shot glass.

Curtain Call

1 part Jägermeister • 1 part whisk(e)y • 1 part Midori

Bow out with this shot. It's so delicious, you may well have to come back for an encore!

method

Put the ingredients in the shaker along with some ice cubes and shake. Strain into a shot glass.

Unleaded

1 part dark rum • 1 part tequila gold

But still plenty of power in this high-octane mix of
dark rum and golden tequila.

method

Put some ice cubes into a shaker and pour in the
rum and tequila. Shake and strain into a shot glass.

Dirty Navel

1 part Triple Sec/Cointreau • 1 part white crème de cacao

You've had a fuzzy navel (page 111), now try a dirty one! This shot is a must for chocolate-lovers!

method

Put some ice cubes into a shaker and pour in the ingredients. Shake well and strain into a shot glass.

Fuzzy Navel

1 part vodka • 1 part peach schnapps
1 part orange juice

The fuzzy bits belong to peaches - peach schnapps in this case!

method

Put the ingredients in the shaker along with some ice cubes and shake. Strain into a shot glass.

Elvis Presley

1 part vodka • 1 part Frangelico
1 part Bailey's Irish Cream • 1 part creme de Banane

The King loved peanut butter and banana sandwiches.

method

Put the ingredients in the shaker along with some ice cubes and shake. Strain into a shot glass.

Fiery Blue Mustang

1 part Akavit • 1 part creme de banane
1 part blue curacao

Go little pony! A gorgeous colour and an amazing
fruit flavour - with a kick!

method

Put some ice cubes into a shaker and pour in the
ingredients. Shake well and strain into a shot glass.

Fireball

1 part ouzo • 1 part coffee liqueur
(Tia maria or Kahlua)

The flavours of an afternoon in a Greek cafe - ouzo,
the pastis of greece, and coffee. A shot that's worth
lingering over a little longer!

method

Put the ouzo and the coffee liqueur in the shaker
along with some ice cubes and shake. Strain into a
shot glass.

Future Dance Squad

1 part sloe gin • 1 part dry vermouth

Start a new dance craze after a couple of these gloriously flavoured combinations of sloe gin and dry vermouth.

method

Put the sloe gin and vermouth into the shaker along with some ice cubes and shake. Strain into a shot glass.

Four Horsemen

· I part tequila · I part Sambuca · I part light rum
I part Jagermeister

A devastating – but not Apocalyptical – combination of tequila, Sambuca, rum and Jagermeister. A flavour for each rider!

method

Pour the ingredients in the shaker along with some ice cubes and shake. Strain into a shot glass.

Freddy Kreuger

1 part Sambuca • 1 part Jagermeister • 1 part vodka

The villain of Nightmare on Elm Street. Now name the actor who played him!

method

Put some ice cubes into a shaker and pour in the Sambuca, vodka and Jagermeister. Shake well and strain into a shot glass.

Flat Tyre

2 parts tequila • 1 part Sambuca Negra

Probably bursts going over the cactus spines! Mexico's finest (tequila) meets Italian Black Sambuca with its very subtle hint of licquorice and coffee.

method

Put some ice cubes into a shaker and pour in the tequila and Sambuca Negra. Shake well and strain into a shot glass.

Green Demon

1 part vodka • 1 part light rum
1 part Midori (melon liqueur) • 1 part lemonade

A chance to use one of the most idiosyncratic liqueurs, the melon-flavoured Midori, which in Japanese means 'green'.

method

In a shaker with 2 or 3 ice cubes, shake the vodka, rum and Midori. Add the lemonade to the shaker. Do not shake but stir twice. Strain into a shot glass.

Gladiator

1 part Southern Comfort • 1 part Amaretto
1 part orange juice • 1 part lemon-lime soda

I'm Spartacus! A couple of these shots and you'll be ready to face combat.

method

Put some ice cubes into a shaker and pour in the Southern Comfort, Amaretto and orange juice. Shake well. Now add the lemon-lime soda and stir. Put the cap back on the shaker and strain the mix into a shot glass.

Uzi Shooter

1 part dry vermouth • 1 part Ricard (or Pernod)
1 part sugar syrup

Highly effective! A really sharp (-tasting) shooter that hits the target every time!

method

Put some ice cubes into a shaker and pour in the vermouth, Ricard and the sugar. Shake well and strain into a shot glass.

Grasshopper Shot

1 part blue curacao • 3 parts cognac (or brandy)

An almost iridescent colour courtesy of the blue curacao, this shot also packs plenty of fire power.

method

Put the blue curacao and the cognac (or brandy) in the shaker along with some ice cubes and shake. Strain into a shot glass.

Greek Fire

I part brandy (Metaxa if possible!) • I part ouzo

Greek fire was an incendiary mix of unknown ingredients used by the ancient Greeks to rain down on their enemies. While the ingredients in this shot are known quantities, it's still a pretty fiery mix!

method

Put the brandy and the ouzo in the shaker along with some ice cubes and shake. Strain into a shot glass.

Greek Revolution

1 part ouzo • 1 part Grenadine

Shout out 'Eloutheria!' (Freedom!) before shooting this gorgeous aniseed-and-fruit-flavoured shot!

method

Put some ice cubes into a shaker and pour in the ouzo and the Grenadine. Shake and strain into a shot glass.

Gumball Shooter

1 part Sambuca • 1 part blue curacao

An aniseed-and-citrus-flavoured shot that's really deceptive! It tastes harmless, but beware the aftershock!

method

Put some ice cubes into a shaker and pour in the Sambuca and blue curacao. Shake and strain into a shot glass.

Ghostbuster

1 part vodka • 1 part Midori • 1 part pineapple juice • 1 part orange juice

Who you gonna call? A wonderfully weird colour courtesy of the melon-flavoured Midori.

method

Put some ice cubes into a shaker and pour in the ingredients. Shake well and strain into a shot glass.

Galactic Ale

1 part vodka • 1 part blue curacao • 1 part lime juice
1 part crème de framboise (raspberry liqueur)

For space cadets everywhere, a chance to explore
new flavours and to seek out new liqueurs.

method

In a shaker with 2 or 3 ice cubes, shake all the ingredients
vigorously. Then strain into a shot glass.

Harley Davidson

1 part Jagermeister • 1 part Midori
1 part Baileys Irish Cream

Hog heaven in a glass! This is a truly inspired combination of flavours. Go on, take the ride of your life!

method

Put the ingredients in the shaker along with some ice cubes and shake. Strain into a shot glass.

Peppermint Pattie

I part white crème de menthe • I part white crème de cacao

Very simple to make, but a wonderful subtle chocolate-mint flavour.

method

Place the ingredients in a shaker with some ice cubes. Shake and strain into a shot glass.

Hazelnut Chill

1 part Frangelico • 1 part pineapple juice
1 part lemonade

Nutty! Frangelico is an Italian liqueur made from wild hazelnuts. It comes in a terrific bottle – shaped like a monk, complete with rope belt!

method

Put some ice cubes into a shaker and pour in the Frangelico and pineapple juice. Shake well, then add the lemonade and stir a couple of times. Strain into a shot glass.

Oh My Gosh

1 measure peach schnapps • 1 measure Amaretto

This is a wonderful winter-time warmer, especially if you've just come in from the cold.

method

Add 2 or 3 ice cubes to the shaker. Pour in the peach schnapps and Amaretto and shake. Strain into a shot glass.

Hay Fever Remedy

1 part vodka • 1 part Southern Comfort
1 part Amaretto • 1 part pineapple juice
Dash of Grenadine

It might not actually cure your hayfever, but it will certainly take your mind off it! Feel better almost instantly, then undo all the good by having a second shot!

method

Shake all the ingredients with 2 or 3 ice cubes in a shaker. Strain into a shot glass.

Sex Under the Moonlight

1 part vodka • 1 part coffee liqueur
(Tia Maria or Kahlua) • 1 part port • Splash of cream

For the truly romantic! A curious combination of
ingredients, but an amazing flavour.

method

Put some ice cubes into a shaker and pour in the
ingredients. Shake and strain into a shot glass.

Sex on the Beach

I part vodka • I part peach schnapps
I part cranberry juice • I part orange juice

Go on, ask the bartender for this! One of the most famous shots, it has a terrific fruity flavour that can be quite addictive!

method

Put the ingredients in the shaker along with some ice cubes and shake. Strain into a shot glass.

Scorpion Suicide

1 part cherry brandy • 1 part whisk(e)y
1 part Pernod

A real stinger! The famous French pastis, Pernod, gives this shot a slightly 'milky' appearance.

method

Put some ice cubes into a shaker and pour in the ingredients. Shake and strain into a shot glass.

Silver Bullet

1 part gin • 1 part Scotch • Lemon twist

Werewolves beware. Being shot with a silver bullet
is the end!

method

Put some ice cubes into a shaker and pour in the gin and
Scotch. Shake and strain into a shot glass and garnish
with the lemon twist

Teen Wolf

1 part Advocaat • 1 part cherry brandy

Such difficult years! An inspired recipe that makes terrific use of the Dutch brandy and egg-based Advocaat.

method

Put some ice cubes into a shaker and pour in the Advocaat and cherry brandy. Shake and strain into a shot glass.

Golden Russian

1 part vodka • 1 part Galliano

A tasty mix of vodka and Galliano, a vanilla-and-herb-flavoured liqueur named after an Italian general.

method

Put some ice cubes into a shaker and pour in the vodka and Galliano. Shake well and strain into a shot glass.

Waterloo Shooter

I part Mandarine Napoleon • I part spiced rum
I part orange juice

For when you put Abba records on! Waterloo, the site of the battle between the French and the English, is in Belgium, the home of Mandarine Napoleon.

method

Put the ingredients in the shaker along with some ice cubes and shake. Strain into a shot glass.

Squished Smurf

1 part peach schnapps • 1 part Baileys Irish Cream
1 part blue curacao • Dash of Grenadine

Remember those annoying creatures? Well, they're squished now. A 'strange'-coloured shot, but a fantastic taste.

method

Put some ice cubes into a shaker and pour in the ingredients. Shake and strain into a shot glass.

Red Beard

1 part Captain Morgan spiced rum • 1 part Malibu
Splash of lemon-lime soda • Splash of Grenadine

For pirates everywhere! A perfect blend of spiced and coconut rums with a hint of tropical fruit.

method

Put the ingredients (except the lemon-lime soda) in the shaker along with some ice cubes and shake. Strain into a shot glass and top with the lomon-lime soda.

Rick

1 part Sambuca • 1 part orange juice

Of all the bars... I doubt that Bogart served these in his *Casablanca* bar – maybe if he had, Bergman would have never got on that plane!

method

Put some ice cubes into a shaker and pour in the Sambuca and orange juice. Shake and strain into a shot glass.

Redneck Marine

1 part Jagermeister • 1 part whiskey • 1 part akvavit

Your country needs you! A great opportunity to crack open the Akvavit.

method

Put some ice cubes into a shaker and pour in the Jagermeister, whiskey and akvavit. Shake and strain into a shot glass.

Turkey Shoot

1 part Wild Turkey • 1 part anisette

Shoot that bird! Wild Turkey straight Kentucky bourbon is available as both 43% abv and 50.5% abv, known as Wild Turkey 101. Choose your weapon!

method

Put the ingredients in the shaker along with some ice cubes and shake. Strain into a shot glass.

Pineapple Bomb

I part Southern Comfort • I part Triple Sec (or Cointreau) I part pineapple juice

Surely thaat's a hand grenade? The peach flavour of the Southern Comfort and the orange of the triple Sec are complemented by pineapple juice.

method

Put the ingredients in the shaker along with some ice cubes and shake. Strain into a shot glass.

Purple Rain

1 part vodka • 1 part blue curacao
Splash cranberry juice

Homage to the 'artist formerly known as Prince',
who would have loved this gorgeous-tasting and
coloured shot.

method

Put some ice cubes into a shaker and pour in the vodka,
curacao and cranberry juice. Shake and strain into a shot
glass.

Poison Apple

1 part Calvados or applejack • 1 part vodka

Only Snow White should beware this fruity treat. The vodka is the 'poison' (vodka is a neutral spirit that is essentially 'flavourless') and the apple comes from Calvados or Applejack – apple brandies.

method

Put some ice cubes into a shaker and pour in the vodka and the Calvados/applejack. Shake and strain into a shot glass.

Porto Covo

1 part vodka • 1 part absinthe (or Pernod)
1 part Malibu • 1 part crème de banane

Sounds like a nice place! Absinthe is a remarkably potent spirit – it was known by artists in the 19th century as 'the green fairy'. Too many of these and you'll see them too!

method

Put the vodka, absinthe, crème de banane and Malibu in the shaker along with some ice cubes and shake. Strain into a shot glass.

Rabbit Punch

I part Campari • I part dark crème de cacao
I part Baileys Irish Cream • I part Malibu

Specially designed for mad March hares: say 'white rabbit, white rabbit' as you raise your shot. Take a second shot and see if you can still pronounce the 'r' in rabbit!

method

Put the ingredients in the shaker along with some ice cubes and shake. Strain into a shot glass.

Paddy's Day Special

1 part green crème de menthe • 1 part Triple Sec or Cointreau • 1 part Midori

Celebrate St Patricks day with this one! A suitably green-coloured shot, but the flavours are far removed from the 'Emerald Isle'.

method

Put the ingredients in the shaker along with some ice cubes and shake. Strain into a shot glass.

Purple Hooter

I part vodka (try a citrus vodka if you want!)
I part Triple Sec or Cointreau • Dash of crème de
framboise (raspberry liqueur)

A gorgeous colour and a great taste, too. A distictly
fruity shot – full of oranges and raspberries!

method

Shake the ingredients with 2 or 3 ice cubes in a shaker
and strain into a shot glass.

Pistol Shot

1 part Triple Sec or Cointreau • 1 part cherry brandy
1 part apricot brandy

Goes down great guns. A sweet-tasting shot packed
with fruit flavours.

method

Put the ingredients in the shaker along with some ice
cubes and shake. Strain into a shot glass.

Woo-Woo Shooter

1 part vodka • 1 part peach schnapps
1 part cranberry juice

Once known as the Teeny-Weeny Woo-Woo, the original Woo-Woo came to fame in the 1980s as a highball (long) drink. Here it is as a shooter: prepared to be wooed and wowed!

method

Shake with 2 or 3 ice cubes in a shaker then strain into a shot glass.

Paralyser

1 part Tia Maria or Kahlúa • 1 part vodka
1 part cola • 1 part milk

You might only need two to get a result. Yes, it contains milk and cola – but don't overlook the vodka and coffee liqueur!

method

Put some ice cubes into a shaker and pour in the coffee liqueur, the vodka and the milk. Shake, pour in the cola and stir, then strain into a shot glass.

Ponderosa

1 part akvavit • 1 part orangeade

Bonanza! A very simple, but highly effective, shot. Why not try Norwegian akvavit? Lysholm Linie akvavit has crossed the equator twice by ship!

method

Chill the akvavit by shaking it with some ice. Pour the orangeade into the shaker and stir. Strain into a shot glass.

Trick Shots
Fancy, Coloured, Layered Shots for Steady Hands!

Bartenders call these drinks pousse-cafés – 'after coffee'. In the last 20 years or so, pousse-cafés have enjoyed something of a renaissance, in the form of shooters.

A pousse-café is a series of liqueurs and spirits (and other ingredients such as cream!) floating on top of each other in the glass in a sort of quaffable rainbow! In this section you'll find some easy ones – with two layers – along with some three-layered drinks. The trick is that different liqueurs have different weights, and this means they have to be poured in ascending order of lightness. Often, the level at the top is a spirit.

The technique requires a steady hand: each liqueur needs to be poured very slowly over the back (the rounded side) of a spoon. It helps to decant the liqueurs into small jugs, as this makes it a lot easier to control the flow of alcohol than from a full-sized bottle. You can cheat, though, and use a turkey baster! Gently dribble the liqueur over the spoon, drop by drop to form a layer. It's also a lot easier to create neat divisions between the different levels if you select glasses with straight sides: pousse-café glasses are by nature tall and narrow, a bit like tubes!

Don't worry if you end up with a drink that's a little wobbly – it happens! The beauty of these shot recipes is that if the layering goes wrong, you can shake or stir the drink, drink it straight up or on the rocks. So have fun!

Beam Me Up Scotty

1 part Kahlua • 1 crème de banane
1 part Baileys Irish Cream

Be transported! Bananas and cream with a hint of
coffee in a glowing tower of tastes.

method

Layer the ingredients in the glass in the order shown by
pouring each of the ingredients slowly over the back of
a spoon. Alternatively, shake with ice and strain into the
glass.

Advosary

1 part Advocaat • 2 parts maraschino

Legend says that the Dutch invented Advocaat after travellers in the East Indies discovered a native drink made out of the pulp of avocado pears. Others maintain that the brandy-and-egg liqueur acquired its name for its ability to loosen the tongue and enable even the most quiet to speak like an advocate (lawyer)!

method

Layer the ingredients in the glass in the order shown. Alternatively, you can shake with ice then strain into a glass.

After Eight

1 part white crème de menthe • 1 part coffee liqueur (Tia Maria or Kahlua) • 1 part Baileys Irish Cream

Coffee and mints are the traditional post-prandial offerings. Here they are, all in a glass!

method

Layer the ingredients in the glass in the order shown by pouring each of the ingredients slowly over the back of a spoon. Alternatively, shake with ice and strain into the glass.

After Nine

*1 part Kahlua • 1 part peach schnapps
1 part Baileys Irish Cream*

Still peckish? Try this tasty layer-cake of coffee,
peaches and cream.

method

Layer the ingredients in the glass in the order shown by
pouring each of the ingredients slowly over the back of
a spoon.

B-52

(classic) 1 part Kahlua • 1 part Baileys Irish Cream
1 part Grand Marnier
(variation) 1 part Kahlua • 1 part Baileys Irish Cream
1 part Cointreau

This drink is pretty famous, although many recipe books give different quantities for the ingredients, and even different ingredients depending on the author's particular preference for a liqueur! We'll keep it simple and use equal measures.

method

Pour each of the ingredients slowly over the back of a spoon into the glass in the order shown. Alternatively shake with ice and strain into the glass.

For a B-53: 1 part Kahlua, 1 part Sambuca, 1 part Grand marnier. layer in the glass in the order shown.

Blow Job

No.1: 1 part coffee liqueur • 1 part Amaretto • Whipped cream

No.2: 1 part coffee liqueur • 1 part Baileys • Whipped cream

No.3: 1 part coffee liqueur • 1 part vodka • Whipped cream

No.4: 1 part Baileys • 1 part creme de banane • Whipped cream

No.5: 1 part Baileys • 1 part Grand marnier • Whipped cream

No self-respecting shooter book would be complete without this! In fact there are several variations on this theme. Some bars insist you also drink these without using your hands! We've shown No. 3 here.

method

Pour each of the ingredients slowly over the back of a spoon into the glass in the order shown. Finally float the whipped cream on top. Alternatively, stir the ingredients together with ice, strain and then float the cream on top.

Book Me An Ambulance

I part yellow Chartreuse • I part cherry brandy
I part absinthe

This shooter contains some pretty strong stuff, so
you may just need that ride after all!

method

Pour each of the ingredients slowly over the back of
a spoon into the glass in the order shown.

For My Next Trick

1 part Grenadine • 1 part dark crème de cacao
1 part green crème de menthe • 1 part blue curaçao
1 part maraschino • 1 part green Chartreuse

Once you've got the hang of layering drinks you can have fun with the ingredients and colours and make a rainbow! Try this six shooter for fun!

method

Starting with the Grenadine, gently pour each of the ingredients over the back of a spoon into the glass in the order given.

Chocolate Almond

I part dark crème de cacao • I part Amaretto
I part Baileys Irish Cream

Better than chewing, no nutty bits stuck in your
teeth!

method
Layer the ingredients into a glass by pouring them in
the order shown over the back of a spoon.

Blue Eyed Blonde

1 part crème de banane • 1 part blue curacao
1 part Baileys Irish Cream

It (almost) looks like one! This bombshell's eyes are
blue curacao, but if you prefer your blondes with
green eyes, try Midori instead!

method

Pour each of the ingredients slowly over the back of
a spoon into the glass in the order shown.

Pipeline

1 part vodka • 1 part tequila

Clears blocked pipes for certain! This is a great shot if you've got unsteady hands – the two layers are almost imperceptible – except on the tongue!

method
Layer in a shot glass and shoot!

Reality Twist

1 part blue curacao • 1 part Amaretto

Enter a different dimension with a couple of shots of this! The 'blue sky' lies underneath the 'dark Earth' in this upside-down world!

method

Pour the blue curacao into the shot glass and gently float the Amaretto on top.

Liquid Asphalt

1 part Sambuca • 1 part Jagermeister

For a realistic approach, try using Sambuca Negra (black Sambuca) to make the asphalt!

method

Float the Jagermeister on top of the Sambuca and shoot.

Dagger

1 part white crème de cacao • 1 part peach schnapps
1 part tequila

Is this a dagger I see before me? Lady Macbeth had
obviously had one too many!

method

Layer the ingredients in the shot glass by pouring
them in the order given slowly over the back of a
spoon.

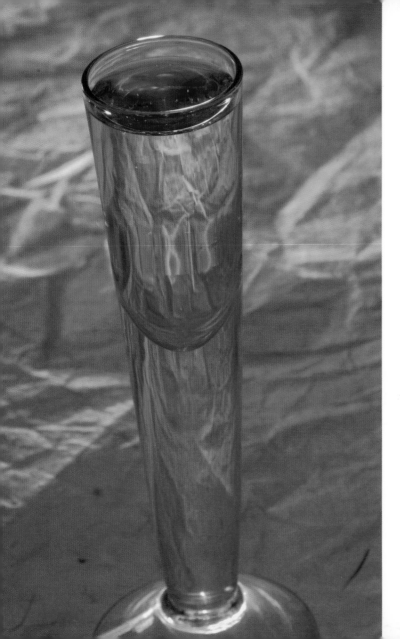

Lovelorn

1 part apricot brandy • 1 part dry vermouth

Shoot yourself on February 15th! And live to fight another day. A very simple shot, yet very effective at mending broken hearts.

method

Float the dry vermouth on top of the apricot brandy.

P.H.

1 part Amaretto • 1 part pineapple juice
1 part Southern Comfort • Dash of lime juice

Perfectly balanced: not too sweet not too sour!
A fruit-and-nut-flavoured shot that looks a little
like a bumble bee.

method

Layer the ingredients in the shot glass by pouring
them in the order given slowly over the back of a
spoon.

Caramilk

2 parts white crème de cacao
1 part crème de banane • 1 part Tia Maria or Kahlua

A sweet mix of chocolate, banana and coffee flavours. In a word: lunch.

method

Layer the ingredients into a glass by pouring them gently in the order given over the back of a spoon. If it all goes wrong, just stir it together, it's still yummy!

Blue Thrill

I part lemon juice • I part blue curacao

A good pousse-café to start off with, and a nice fruity taste too.

method

Float the blue curacao on top of the lemon juice.

The Devil You Don't Know

1 part dark crème de cacao • 1 part Jägermeister

Ever wondered what you were missing when you opted for the Devil You Know? Now is your chance to find out in this chocolate-flavoured shot!

method

Pour each of the ingredients slowly over the back of a spoon into the glass in the order shown.

Coconut Cream Pie

1 part chilled Malibu • Whipped cream

A real easy one! If you can't manage this, stick to shaken shots! If you've a sweet tooth, this shot will be ideal for you.

method

Chill the Malibu – either stir or shake with some ice – then strain into the glass. Float the whipped cream on top.

Cross-cultural Black Russian

I part Kahlua • I part Tia Maria • I part vodka

The original Black Russian was a mix of vodka and either Kahlua or Tia Maria. This Cross-cultural version shows the eclectic mix of contemporary culture. Either that, or we're just being greedy!

method

Pour each of the ingredients slowly over the back of a spoon into the glass in the order shown. Alternatively, shake with ice and strain into the glass.

City Hot Shot

1 part Grenadine • 1 part blue curacao
1 part Triple Sec

For when the markets close and the deals have been done, try this colourful citrus shot.

method

Layer the ingredients into a glass by pouring them gently in the order given over the back of a spoon.

Green Fly Shooter

I part Midori • I part green crème de menthe

It's small, green and can wreak havoc among tender shoot(er)s! This is an inspired flavour combination – melon and mint – and a gorgeous colour, too!

method

Pour each of the ingredients slowly over the back of a spoon into the glass in the order shown. Alternatively, shake with ice and strain into the glass.

Electric Banana

I part crème de banane • I part tequila

It's a banana with a mains voltage. The first flavour to hit your tomgue is tequila, followed swiftly by banana.

method

Pour the crème de banane into the glass, then gently pour in the tequila so it floats on top.

Elphino

1 part Sambuca • 1 part Triple Sec

A very simple yet delicious aniseed-citrus combination. You can use golden Sambuca or Negra (black) for dramatic effect.

method

Pour the Sambuca into the glass and gently float the Triple Sec on top.

The Girl Mum Warned You About

1 part Grenadine • 1 part Midori • 1 part blue curacao
1 part Triple Sec/Cointreau • 1 part rum

She can be tricky, and she may let you down, but
she's worth trying for!

method

Pour the ingredients gently over the bacl of a spoon
in the order shown.

Doucet Devil

1 part crème de banane • 2 parts Amaretto
1 part Southern Comfort

Not quite so devilish! Very softly coloured layers of golden liqueurs, but three very distinct flavours.

method
Pour each of the ingredients slowly over the back of a spoon into the glass in the order shown.

Necrophiliac

I part Advocaat • I part blue curacao

A strange pastime for strange people. This is a really tasty shot: citrus at the top and creamy brandy at the base.

method

Pour the Advocaat into the glass, and then float the blue curacao on the top.

Hot to Trot

1 part cinnamon schnapps • Dash of lime juice
1 part tequila

This is a terrific spicy shot, if you dare! The dash of lime juice between the two 'hard' layers really kicks your tastebuds!

method

Pour the schnapps into the glass and layer the dash of lime juice on top. Gently float the tequila on top and shoot.

Tequila Mockingbird

1 part Amaretto • 1 part tequila

Great pun, great shooter! The taste of tequila combines perfectly with the almond-flavoured Amaretto.

method

Layer in a shot glass.

White Lightning

1 part tequila • 1 part white crème de cacao

Tequila and chocolate, the food and drink of the Aztec gods. Tequila was 'discovered' by the Aztecs after their gods sent a lightning-bolt from heaven which landed on an agave plant and 'cooked' it into the spirit's drink!

method

Pour the tequila in the shot glass and float the white crème de cacao on top.

B.B.C.

1 part Baileys Irish Cream • 1 part Benedictine
1 part Cointreau

Not, in fact, named after the British Broadcasting Corporation, but a handy mnemonic for the ingredients.

method

Layer the ingredients in the glass, pouring them into the glass in the order given. For a B.B.G. substitute Grand Marnier for the Cointreau.

Battered, Bruised & Bleeding

*I part Grenadine • I part blue curacao
I part Midori*

The battered part is the blue curacao, the bruised is the green Midori, and the bleeding the red of the Grenadine. The only thing that is assaulted, though, is your tongue!

method

Layer the ingredients in the glass, pouring them into the glass in the order given.

Red Hot

Dash of hot sauce • 1 part tequila
1 part cinnamon schnapps

A real hot shot! If you're really daring, substitute a dash of wasabi for the hot sauce!

method

Put the hot sauce into the bottom of the shot glass. Next pour in the tequila, then layer the cinnamon schnapps on top.

E.T.

*1 part Midori • 1 part Baileys Irish Cream
1 part vodka*

Phone home and say you'll be late! In most layered shots, Baileys makes the topmost layer and forms a creamy head. Try it here sandwiched between Midori and vodka.

method

Layer the ingredients in the shot glass by pouring them in the order given slowly over the back of a spoon.

Late Bloomer

I part apricot brandy • I part Triple Sec • I part rum

Better late than never! A very tasty combination of rum, oranges and apricots in subtly coloured layers.

method

Pour the apricot brandy into the glass, then layer on the Triple Sec and float the rum on top.

Fisherman's Wharf

1 part Amaretto • 1 part Triple Sec
1 part Courvoisier/cognac

A great shot for when you're sitting on a dock by the bay. This original recipe uses Courvoisier cognac.

method

Layer the ingredients in the glass in the order given above.

Stormy Weather

1 part Sambuca Negra • 1 part whipped cream

The white whipped cream floating on black
Sambuca makes this shot look like thunder clouds
in a glass! It's a fun shot and a great alternative
to 'after-dinner' coffee.

method

Pour the Sambuca Negra into the glass to create the
dark sky. Float the whipped cream on top to make
clouds!

Streetcar

1 part dark crème de cacao • 1 part Baileys Irish Cream
1 part apricot brandy

A streetcar that should be named Desire. This shot contains the flavours of chocolate, coffee, cream and apricots with whiskey and brandy undertones.

method

Layer the ingredients in the order shown in the shot glass.

Redback Shooter

I part Advocaat • I part Sambuca

An interesting combination. You can use black or golden Sambuca – and why not try some flavoured Advocaats too? Mocha and chocolate are available!

method

Pour the Advocaat into the glass and then gently pour in the Sambuca so that it floats on top.

Six Shooters
Party Shots and Jellies

No matter what you are celebrating, serving drinks is one of the best ways of getting the party going. Be warned, though, that while alcohol certainly makes for fun, it can also bring out the worst in people, including the hosts!

Party shots are a great way of keeping the party on track: three or four shots per person are plenty, and if they are interspersed with conversation, food and party games and quizzes, the emphasis is on a good time, rather than just drinking.

In this section, you'll find recipes for party shots and shooters, because they contain a fair number of ingredients and are actually easier to make in volume than as individual drinks. In general, the recipes will make around six shots, which is why I've called them Six Shooters! Just shake them and pour them into shot glasses and hand them around. Mixing shots in this way means that, as host, you can keep tabs on the number of shots guests have had. Remember, each shot glass holds around 5.7 cl/ 2 fl oz and around half of the shot, if not a little more, will be made up of spirits and liqueurs with pretty high levels of alcohol by volume! You can use a bar jigger or a shot glass as a measure, but don't forget that because you'll be shaking the ing--redients with ice you'll be increasing the volume of the final mix. It's a good idea to practise first using plain water to check the measure, that way you won't waste any of the precious spirits and liqueurs!.

Alongside the Six Shooter recipes, you'll also find recipes for some types of shooters that have recently become really popular in bars and at parties: these are gelatine shots, variously called jelly shots, Jell-o shots (after the proprietary brand of North American fruit-flavoured gelatine) and jiggelos.

While contemporary gelatine shots started their lives in the 1980s as novelty drinks favoured by college students, the origins of flavouring gelatine with alcohol go back to the early years of the 20th century. In the United States, one Otis Glidden produced a gelatine product that included a small glass vial of flavouring suspended in alcohol. This, the first gelatine shooter, was on sale for just a few years, until prohibition was introduced! In recent years, and riding on the crest of the wave of interest in classic cocktails, creative bartenders across the world have transformed the gelatine shot into a rather trendy cocktail.

You don't drink gelatine shots, you eat them. You can do this with a spoon, or you can squeeze them out of the little disposable cups, slurping and sucking them into your mouth! Disposable plastic shot glasses and jiggelo cups are now widely available. They are sometimes called soufflé cups and you can get them at most good retailers or buy on-line. For the ultimate in luxury, you could even create a gelatine shot in an edible chocolate cup. Look in the home-baking section in supermarkets for these! If you don't have any containers, you can always set them in ice cube trays and rubber moulds, or even in baking pans/trays and then cut them into mouth-sized cubes! You'll find more information about gelatine shots, such as using unflavoured gelatine and vegetarian gelatine.

Sexy Alligator

1 measure Malibu • 1 measure Midori
1 measure Jagermeister • 1 measure crème de framboise
(raspberry liqueur) • 1 measure pineapple juice

Tropical, green and a big bite! This is a really terrific combination of flavours: coconut, melon, raspberries, pineapple and herbs.

method

Put some ice cubes into the shaker. Using a jigger or shot glass, measure out equal amounts of the ingredients and pour them into the shaker. Shake and then strain into 6 shot glasses. If, for some strange reason you'd rather have Sex with an Alligator, simply omit the Malibu!

Chevy

1 measure Southern Comfort • 1 measure Triple Sec
1 measure Amaretto • ½ measure orange juice
½ measure pineapple juice • ½ measure Grenadine
½ measure lemon-lime soda

Cruise in a classic, but dont drink and drive! This fruit-flavoured shot is more powerful than you think!

method

Put some ice cubes into the shaker. Using a jigger or shot glass, measure out equal amounts of the ingredients, except for the lemon-lime soda, and pour them into the shaker. Shake, pour in the lemon-lime soda and stir, and then strain into 6 shot glasses.

Unholy Water

1 measure gin • 1 measure akvavit
1 measure spiced rum • 1 measure tequila
1 measure vodka

But a heavenly taste! There are no fruit juices or mixers in this drink, just plain old alcohol, so watch how many you shoot, or things might just get a little hellish!

method

Put some ice cubes into the shaker. Using a jigger or shot glass, measure out equal amounts of the ingredients and pour them into the shaker. Shake and then strain into 6 shot glasses.

Pink Belly

1 measure Jim Beam bourbon • 1 measure Amaretto
1 measure sloe gin • 1 measure Baileys Irish Cream
1 measure lemon-lime soda

After a couple of shots of this, you'll find some folks
can't help showing you theirs!

method

Put some ice cubes into the shaker. Using a jigger or shot
glass, carefully measure out equal amounts of the
ingredients, except for the lemon-lime soda, and pour
them into the shaker. Shake, pour in the lemon-lime soda
and stir, and then strain into 6 shot glasses.

Illusion

1 measure Malibu • 1 measure Midori
1 measure vodka • 1 measure Cointreau
½ measure pineapple juice

It's magic! This pale green delight gets its colour from Midori and its slightly coconut flavour from Malibu.

method

Put some ice cubes into the shaker. Using a jigger or shot glass, carefully measure out equal amounts of the ingredients and pour them into the shaker. Shake well and then strain into 6 shot glasses.

Memory Loss

1 measure crème de banane • 1 measure vodka
1 measure crème de framboise (raspberry liqueur)
1 measure cranberry juice • 1 measure orange juice

Blame this if you can't remember what you did last night! Be warned, its fruity flavour may make you forget it's alcohol.

method

Put some ice cubes into the shaker. Using a jigger or shot glass, carefully measure out equal amounts of the ingredients and pour them into the shaker. Shake well and then strain into 6 shot glasses.

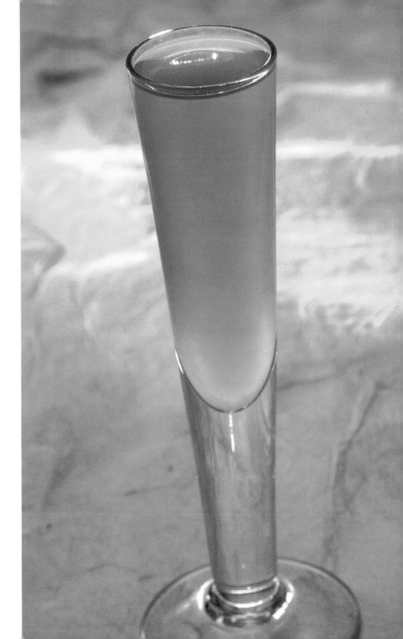

Death By Sex

1 measure vodka • 1 measure Triple Sec
1 measure sloe gin • 1 measure peach schnapps
1 measure Amaretto • 1 measure Southern Comfort
½ measure cranberry juice • ½ measure orange

What a way to go! A real fruity confection, so you'll 'die' with a smile on your face.

method

Put some ice cubes into the shaker. Using a jigger or shot glass, carefully measure out equal amounts of the ingredients and pour them into the shaker. Shake and then strain into 6 shot glasses. Say a prayer!

Memory Loss

1 measure crème de banane • 1 measure vodka
1 measure crème de framboise (raspberry liqueur)
1 measure cranberry juice • 1 measure orange juice

Blame this if you can't remember what you did last night! Be warned, its fruity flavour may make you forget it's alcohol.

method

Put some ice cubes into the shaker. Using a jigger or shot glass, carefully measure out equal amounts of the ingredients and pour them into the shaker. Shake well and then strain into 6 shot glasses.

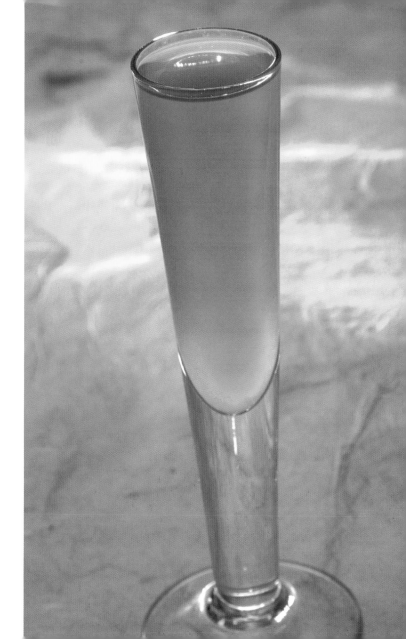

Hurricane Hugo

1 measure vodka • 1 measure Amaretto
1 measure sloe gin • ½ measure Southern Comfort
½ measure Midori • 1 measure orange juice
1 measure cranberry juice

Batten down the hatches, its devastating! There are four measures of booze in this shot, so be prepared for a storm!

method

Put some ice cubes into the shaker. Using a jigger or shot glass, carefully measure out equal amounts of the ingredients and pour them into the shaker. Shake well and then strain into 6 shot glasses.

The Green Monster

*1 measure vodka • 1 measure Cointreau
1 measure Midori • 1 measure peach schnapps
1 measure Southern Comfort*

Remember the old adage: you are what you eat! This beautiful delicately coloured shot is a power-packed punch.

method

Put some ice cubes into the shaker. Using a jigger or shot glass, carefully measure out equal amounts of the ingredients and pour them into the shaker. Shake and then strain into 6 shot glasses. If you turn into the Incredible Hulk, it's your own fault – you've had one too many shooters!

Johnny on the Beach

1 measure vodka • 1 measure Midori
1 measure crème de cassis • 1 measure pineapple juice
1 measure orange juice • 1 measure grapefruit juice
1 measure cranberry juice

This is a classic among shots and everyone has their own version of the origin of the name. But everyone agrees that it tastes fantastic!

method

Put some ice cubes into the shaker. Using a jigger or shot glass, carefully measure out equal amounts of the ingredients and pour them into the shaker. Shake and then strain into 6 shot glasses.

Inebriator

1 measure vodka • 1 measure Triple Sec
1 measure gin • 1 measure Amaretto
3 measures pineapple juice

Does exactly what it says on the label.
The pineapple juice and the almond-flavour of
the Amaretto can be deceptive – so go easy on
these shots!

method

Put some ice cubes into the shaker. Using a jigger or shot
glass, carefully measure out equal amounts of the
ingredients and pour them into the shaker. Shake and
then strain into 6 shot glasses.

Liquid Cocaine

No. 1 1 measure tequila • 1 measure vodka • 1 measure gin
1 measure light rum • 1 measure akvavit • 1 measure lemon-lime soda
No. 2 1 measure vodka • 1 measure Amaretto • 1 measure Southern
Comfort • 1 measure Cointreau • 1 measure pineapple juice

A number of recipes go by this name – just goes to
show, you can never tell what's really in them. And
all of it hard stuff! The one in the picture is the No.1.

method

No 1: Put some ice cubes into the shaker. Using a jigger
or shot glass, carefully measure out equal amounts of the
ingredients, except for the lemon-lime soda, and pour
them into the shaker. Shake, pour in the lemon-lime soda
and stir, and then strain into 6 shot glasses.

No 2: Put some ice cubes into the shaker. Using a jigger
or shot glass, carefully measure out equal amounts of the
ingredients and pour them into the shaker. Shake well
and then strain into 6 shot glasses.

Grapevine

I measure cognac or brandy
I measure apricot brandy • I measure crème de banane
I measure maraschino • I measure Triple Sec

You heard it through the grapevine. The name refers to the various 'brandies' in here, but only cognac is a true grape brandy.

method

Put some ice cubes into the shaker. Using a jigger or shot glass, carefully measure out equal amounts of the ingredients and pour them into the shaker. Shake and then strain into 6 shot glasses.

Laser Beam

2 measures Southern Comfort • 2 measures Midori
1 measure Amaretto • 1 measure Triple Sec
2 measures pineapple juice

Very sci-fi! Perfect for mad scientists, and a terrific 'neon' colour.

method

Put some ice cubes into the shaker. Using a jigger or shot glass, carefully measure out equal amounts of the ingredients and pour them into the shaker. Shake well and then strain into 6 shot glasses.

Lava Lamp

1 measure Tia Maria or Kahlua
1 measure crème de fraise (strawberry liqueur)
1 measure Frangelico • 6 drops of Advocaat

Remember those mesmerising, swirling blobs of colour floating in a glass lantern? Well, they're back!

method

Put some ice cubes into the shaker and using the jigger or shot glass, carefully measure out the ingredients and pour them all, except for the Advocaat, into the shaker. Shake and strain into 6 shot glass. Now put a single drop of Advocaat into the centre of each shot and make mini lava lamps!

G.T.O.

*1 measure rum • 1 measure gin • 1 measure vodka
1 measure Southern Comfort • 1 measure Amaretto
1 measure Grenadine • 1 measure orange juice*

A supercharged shooter. The gorgeous colour is created by the Grenadine, a pink syrup made from pomegranates.

method

Put some ice cubes into the shaker. Using a jigger or shot glass, carefully measure out equal amounts of the ingredients and pour them into the shaker. Shake and then strain into 6 shot glasses. Mirror, signal, manoeuvre.

Pants on Fire

1 measure vodka • 1 measure crème de fraise
(strawberry liqueur) • 1 measure crème de banane
1 measure orange juice

Best drunk during a game of Truth or Dare, at
least you can then shout the old playground taunt:
'liar, liar, pants on fire'. Or did I go to a particularly
rough school?

method

Put some ice cubes into the shaker. Using a jigger or shot
glass, carefully measure out equal amounts of the
ingredients and pour them into the shaker. Shake well
and then strain into 6 shot glasses.

Jiggelos: Gelatine Shots

This is the basic recipe for 18-20 shots, which will happily serve 4 to 6 people. To make things simple in the recipes, we'll call the measure for the hot water 1 part, and the equivalent amount of spirits/liqueurs and/or juices 1 part.

- 1 packet jelly (see flavour combinations, or use unflavoured gelatine if you prefer shots that are a little less sweet)
- hot water to dissolve the jelly: see the instructions on the package for the quantity
- the same quantity of your favourite spirit/liqueur and juices (or combination of spirits/liqueurs and juices) to make up the finished volume
- 20 disposable plastic shot glasses or disposable cups

Because of the different natures of spirits and liqueurs, some will set faster than others, so prepare your jiggelos well in advance of your party! Once you've got the hang of jiggelos, you can have real fun. You can make just about any cocktail or shooter recipe into a gelatine shot. You can layer them too: just let one level set in the fridge first before you add the next layer(s). If you want a clear level or layer in a jiggelo, then it's best to use unflavoured gelatine. Unflavoured gelatine gives you a neutral base which you can infuse with flavours from fresh juices and liqueurs, without adding any extra sweetness. The only liqueurs that don't work so well in jiggelos are the cream-based liqueurs such as Baileys Irish Cream, which tends to separate. However, while the visual effect may not be what you want, it won't affect the flavour.

Lemonhead

1 packet lemon-flavoured jelly • 1 part hot water to
dissolve (see packet for quantity) • 1 part vodka

A citrus-vodka-flavoured jelly-shot that's easy to
make and fun to eat.

method

In a heat-proof bowl, break or cut the lemon gelatine
into cubes. Boil some water and measure out the
quantity stated on the jelly packet required to dissolve
the jelly. Stir until the jelly is dissolved. Let this mix cool.
Pour in the vodka, an amount equal to the water, and stir
to combine it well. Pour into plastic shot glasses or
disposable cups and chill in the fridge until firm.

Mexican Jumping Jelly Bean

1-2 envelopes unflavoured gelatine (enough to make 18-20
shots, see packs for quantities)
1 part hot water to dissolve (see packet for quantity)
½ part Kahlua • ½ part tequila • Good splash of Grenadine

Jump for joy after tasting this Mexican delight

method

Following the instructions on the package for quantities and methods, dissolve the gelatine with the appropriate amount of hot water and stir well to dissolve. Let this cool. When cool, measure out the tequila and Kahlua. The total amount of these should equal the amount of hot water used to dissolve the gelatine. Mix together the tequila and Kahlua. Shake with a few ice cubes if you like, then strain and pour into the gelatine mix. Stir well to combine, then pour into individual shot glasses and chill in the fridge until firm.

Slow Comfortable French Jelly Bean

1-2 envelopes unflavoured gelatine (enough to make 18-20 shots, see packs for quantities)
1 part hot water to dissolve (see packet for quantity)
¼ part sloe gin • ¼ part Pernod • ¼ part Southern Comfort

Slow from sloe gin; comfortable from Southern Comfort; French from Pernod.

method

Following the instructions on the package for quantities and methods, dissolve the gelatine with the appropriate amount of hot water and stir well to dissolve. Let this cool. When cool, measure out the sloe gin, Pernod and Southern Comfort. The total amount of these should equal the amount of hot water used to dissolve the gelatine. Mix together the sloe gin, Pernod and Southern Comfort. Shake with a few ice cubes if you like, then strain and pour into the gelatine mix. Stir well to combine, then pour into individual shot glasses and chill in the fridge until firm.

Italian Jelly Bean

*1-2 envelopes unflavoured gelatine (enough to make
18-20 shots, see packs for quantities)
1 part hot water to dissolve (see packet for quantity)
½ part sambuca • ½ part Galliano • ½ part Grenadine*

The Italians in here are Sambuca and Galliano – with a little Grenadine added for good measure!

method

Following the instructions on the package for quantities and methods, dissolve the gelatine with the appropriate amount of hot water and stir well to dissolve. Let this cool. When cool, measure out the sambuca, Galliano, and Grenadine. The total amount of these should equal the amount of hot water used to dissolve the gelatine. Mix together the sambuca, Galliano and Grenadine. Shake with a few ice cubes if you like, then strain and pour into the gelatine mix. Stir well to combine, then pour into individual shot glasses and chill in the fridge until firm.

Bean There,
Done That!

Tequila and Amaretto are a surprisingly fine
combination.

method

Following the instructions on the package for quantities
and methods, dissolve the gelatine with the appropriate
amount of hot water and stir well to dissolve. Let this
cool. When cool, measure out the tequila, Amaretto and
Grenadine. The total amount of these should equal the
amount of hot water used to dissolve the gelatine. Mix
together the tequila, Amaretto and Grenadine. Shake
with a few ice cubes if you like, then strain and pour into
the gelatine mix. Stir well to combine, then pour into
individual shot glasses and chill in the fridge until firm.

Flat Tyre, Inflated

1-2 envelopes unflavoured gelatine (enough to make 18-20 shots, see packs for quantities) • 1 part hot water to dissolve (see packet for quantity) • ⅔ part tequila • ⅓ part Sambuca

We met the original flat tyre earlier on. Now try it inflated, as a jiggelo!

method

Following the instructions on the package for quantities and methods, dissolve the gelatine with the appropriate amount of hot water and stir well to dissolve. Let this cool. When cool, measure out the tequila and Sambuca. The total amount of these should equal the amount of hot water used to dissolve the gelatine. Mix together the tequila and Sambuca. Shake with a few ice cubes if you like, then strain and pour into the gelatine mix. Stir well to combine, then pour into individual shot glasses and chill in the fridge until firm.

Wobbling Green Beret

1-2 envelopes unflavoured gelatine (enough to make 18-20 shots, see packs for quantities) • 1 part hot water to dissolve (see packet for quantity) • ½ part vodka • ½ part green crème de menthe

A jelly version of this minty shooter!

method

Following the instructions on the package for quantities and methods, dissolve the gelatine with the appropriate amount of hot water and stir well to dissolve. Let this cool. When cool, measure out the vodka and green crème de menthe. The total amount of these should equal the amount of hot water used to dissolve the gelatine. Mix together the vodka and green crème de menthe. Shake with a few ice cubes if you like, then strain and pour into the gelatine mix. Stir well to combine, then pour into individual shot glasses and chill in the fridge until firm.

Berry Schnapps

1 packet strawberry-flavoured jelly
1 part hot water to dissolve (see packet for quantity)
1 part peach schnapps

Strawberries and peaches are perfect partners in this jiggelo, but you could try any of the variously flavoured schnapps to create your own versions.

method

In a heat-proof bowl, break or cut the strawberry gelatine into cubes. Boil some water and measure out the quantity stated on the jelly packet required to dissolve the jelly. Stir until the jelly is dissolved. Let this mix cool. Pour in the peach schnapps and stir to combine it well. Pour into plastic shot glasses or disposable cups and chill in the fridge until firm.

Jell-a-rita

1 packet lime-flavoured jelly • 1 part hot water to dissolve (see packet for quantity) • 1 part tequila

A jelly version of the famous tequila cocktail, the Margharita, created in 1948 by Danny Herrera for the actress Marjorie King, in Tijuana, Mexico.

method

In a heat-proof bowl, break or cut the lime gelatine into cubes. Boil some water and measure out the quantity stated on the jelly packet required to dissolve the jelly. Stir until the jelly is dissolved. Let this mix cool. Pour in the tequila and stir to combine it well. Pour into plastic shot glasses or disposable cups and chill in the fridge until firm.

Melon Sour

I packet lime-flavoured jelly • I part hot water to dissolve (see packet for quantity) • I part Midori

Sours were drinks that first became popular in the 1850s. This jelly version uses one of the most recent arrivals on the drink scene, Midori.

method

In a heat-proof bowl, break or cut the lime gelatine into cubes. Boil some water and measure out the quantity stated on the jelly packet required to dissolve the jelly. Stir until the jelly is dissolved. Let this mix cool. Pour in the Midori and stir to combine it well. Pour into plastic shot glasses or disposable cups and chill in the fridge until firm.

Tropical Orange

1 packet orange-flavoured jelly • 1 part hot water to dissolve (see packet for quantity) • 1 part Cointreau

Cointreau is a form of Triple Sec or a brandy-based liqueur flavoured with small, bitter oranges from the Caribbean island of Curacoa.

method

In a heat-proof bowl, break or cut the orange gelatine into cubes. Boil some water and measure out the quantity stated on the jelly packet required to dissolve the jelly. Stir until the jelly is dissolved. Let this mix cool. Pour in the Cointreau and stir to combine it well. Pour into plastic shot glasses or disposable cups and chill in the fridge until firm.

Tropical Rum

I packet orange-flavoured jelly • I part hot water to dissolve (see packet for quantity) • I part Malibu

It was Christopher Columbus who took sugar cane to the Caribeean, where it was soon discovered that the sap made fine rum. This tropical jelly shot uses Malibu, a coconut-flavoured rum.

method

In a heat-proof bowl, break or cut the orange gelatine into cubes. Boil some water and measure out the quantity stated on the jelly packet required to dissolve the jelly. Stir until the jelly is dissolved. Let this mix cool. Pour in the Malibu and stir to combine it well. Pour into plastic shot glasses or disposable cups and chill in the fridge until firm.

Gimlet

1 packet lime flavoured jelly • 1 part hot water to
dissolve (see packet for quantity) • 1 part gin

A 'gimlet' is a small, sharp hand tool used to bore holes in wood. The word has also become associated with small, sharp-tasting cocktails.

method

In a heat-proof bowl, break or cut the lime gelatine into cubes. Boil some water and measure out the quantity stated on the jelly packet required to dissolve the jelly. Stir until the jelly is dissolved. Let this mix cool. Pour in the gin, an amount equal to the water and stir to combine it well. Pour into plastic shot glasses or disposable cups and chill in the fridge until firm.

Wobbly Mimosa

I packet orange-flavoured jelly
I part hot water to dissolve (see packet for quantity)
I part flat champagne or flat sparkling white whine

Champagne or sparkling wine lost its fizz? Turn it into a jiggelo!

method

In a heat-proof bowl, break or cut the orange gelatine into cubes. Boil some water and measure out the quantity stated on the jelly packet required to dissolve the jelly. Stir until the jelly is dissolved. Let this mix cool. Pour in the flat champagne or white wine and stir to combine it well. Pour into plastic shot glasses or disposable cups and chill in the fridge until firm.

Sherry Trifle

1 packet strawberry-flavoured jelly
1 part hot water to dissolve (see packet for quantity)
1 part dry sherry • Whipped cream

Sherry is too often overlooked as a drink, so here's a perfect solution: a 'pudding' shot!

method

In a heat-proof bowl, break or cut the strawberry gelatine into cubes. Boil some water and measure out the quantity stated on the jelly packet required to dissolve the jelly. Stir until the jelly is dissolved. Let this mix cool. Pour in the sherry and stir to combine it well. Pour into plastic shot glasses or disposable cups and chill in the fridge until firm. Top each shot with a dollop of whipped cream if you like!

Tricoleurs

Layered jelly shots take a bit of forward planning as you need to chill and set each layer before you add the next one. You can have great fun adding as many different layers, colours and flavours as you like. They're great for big parties: if you make up enough recipe of each colour to make 20 shots, you'll actually be able to make around sixty 3-layered shots! But make sure you've got room in your fridge first! Alternatively, follow the instructions on the gelatine packet regarding quantities/amounts and adjust according to the number of shots you require in total.

Red, White & Blue

Red layer (bottom): 1-2 envelopes flavored red gelatine (enough to make 18-20 shots, see package for quantities) • 1 part hot water to dissolve (see package for quantities) • 1 part Grenadine or sloe gin

Following the instructions on the package for quantities and methods, dissolve the gelatine with the appropriate amount of hot water and stir well to dissolve. Let this cool. Pour in the Grenadine or sloe gin and stir well. Pour the gelatine mix into the shot glass to fill ⅓ of the glass. Chill in the fridge until firm.

White layer (middle): 1-2 envelopes unflavored gelatine (enough to make 18-20 shots, see package to quantities) • 1 part hot water to dissolve (see packet for quantities) • 1 part vodka or Cointreau

Make up the gelatine mix, add the vodka or Cointreau and stir. Pour on top of the firmly set Grenadine or sloe gin layer to fill the glass ⅔ full. Place back in the fridge to chill and set.

Blue layer (top): 1-2 envelopes flavored blue gelatine (enough to make 18-20 shots, see package for quantities) • 1 part hot water to dissolve (see package for quantities) • 1 part blue curacao

Make up the gelatine mix, add the blue curacao and stir. Pour on top of the firmly set clear vodka or Cointreau layer. Place back in the fridge to chill and set.

Red, Gold & Green

Red layer (bottom): 1-2 envelopes unflavoured gelatine (enough to make 18-20 shots, see packs for quantities)• 1 part hot water to dissolve (see packet for quantity)• 1 part Grenadine

Following the instructions on the package for quantities and methods, dissolve the gelatine with the appropriate amount of hot water and stir well to dissolve. Let this cool. Pour in the Grenadine and stir well. Pour the gelatine mix into the shot glass to fill ⅓ of the glass. Chill in the fridge until firm.

Gold layer (middle): 1-2 envelopes unflavoured gelatine (enough to make 18-20 shots, see packs for quantities) • 1 part hot water to dissolve (see packet for quantity) • 1 part gold tequila or Galliano

Make up the gelatine mix, add the gold tequila or Galliano and stir. Pour on top of the firmly set Grenadine layer to fill the glass ⅔ full. Place back in the fridge to chill and set.

Green layer (top): 1-2 envelopes unflavoured gelatine (enough to make 18-20 shots, see packs for quantities) 1 part hot water to dissolve (see packet for quantity) • 1 part Midori

Make up the gelatine mix, add the Midori and stir. Pour on top of the firmly set gold tequila layer to fill the glass. Place back in the fridge to chill and set.

Double Chocolate Mint Stick

Bottom layer: 1-2 envelopes unflavoured gelatine (enough to make 18-20 shots, see packs for quantities) • 1 part milk to dissolve (see packet for quantity and replace the water with an equal amount of milk) • 1 part dark crème de cacao

Add the gelatine to the milk and whisk well. Let the mix sit for 2-3 minutes before bringing it to the boil over a medium heat, whisking frequently to dissolve the gelatine. Let the mixture cool for 10 minutes before adding the dark crème de cacao. Stir to mix. Pour into glasses to fill them ⅓ full and set in the fridge to chill and firm.

Middle layer: 1-2 envelopes unflavoured gelatine (enough to make 18-20 shots, see packs for quantities) • 1 part milk to dissolve • 1 part green crème de menthe

Follow the instructions for the first layer. When the milk and gelatine mix is cool, add the green crème de menthe and stir to mix. Pour on top of the first layer, up to the ⅔ level and put back in the fridge to set.

Top layer: 1-2 envelopes unflavoured gelatine (enough to make 18-20 shots, see packs for quantities) • 1 part milk to dissolve • 1 part white crème de cacao

Follow the instructions as for the first two layers. When the milk and gelatine mix is cool, add the white crème de cacao and stir to mix. Pour this final layer on top of the middle layer, and set back in the fridge to chill and set.

mocktails

Full of flavour and packed with vitamins and minerals, smoothies made from fruit are perhaps the most popular.

-Unlike juices, which lack soluble fibre, smoothies deliver all the natural fibre present in the whole fruit. Fruits are high in natural sugars that your body uses as fuel, which makes them a great way to start the day. But smoothies also make a great mid-morning or afternoon 'pick-me up', an energy-booster after work if you're off to the gym or theatre and don't have the time or the inclination to eat first, and a healthy snack for when you just feel peckish. You will find that some blends are so delicious you can serve them to guests as dessert after dinner, or offer them instead of alcoholic beverages or fizzy sodas at parties.

Fruit smoothies are the perfect way to enjoy seasonal fruits: where possible buy organic fruits so that you can reduce the amounts of potentially harmful chemicals used widely in the commercial production of crops. Nevertheless, you are advised always to wash fruit before slicing, and to peel off the skins. If you have a juicer, you can juice many of the fruit skins too, but a blender won't always be effective in chopping skins. Choose ripe fruits. Under-ripe fruits in smoothies won't have the same juiciness and may taste bitter. Don't worry if a fruit is a little soft, it will still make great smoothies, but avoid fruits that are mouldy or rotten, they are starting to ferment and may cause stomach upsets.

Remember, you can use frozen fruits: this makes smoothies that are not only colder, but a little thicker, at least while they are still frozen! If there is a seasonal surfeit of fresh fruit, peel, seed and stone/pit the fruit and cut it into chunks. Arrange the pieces, or individual berries, washed and patted dry, in a single layer on a baking sheet and freeze them until hard. Transfer the fruit to a re-sealable plastic bag, label and seal. The fruit pieces will keep for up to six months in the freezer.

When fresh fruit is not available, canned fruit is a convenient way to make tasty smoothies. Wherever possible, buy organically grown fruit and fruits canned in their own juice, in water or in apple juice. Fruits canned in heavy sugar syrup are OK, but you

will be adding extra sugar which you probably don't need! You can drain the syrup from the fruit and rinse in cold water: it won't get rid of all the added sugar, but I'd rather have a slightly sweet smoothy than none at all!

Dried fruit can also be used in smoothies: apricots, apples, raisins, prunes, even berries are available in dried forms, but watch out for commercially dried fruits which have been fumigated with sulphur dioxide, a gas that not only destroys the B vitamins – it is also poisonous! Wherever possible, buy unsulphured fruits and wash thoroughly. If you are hooked on health foods, you can buy domestic food dehydrators and dry your own fruits. This makes great commercial and dietary sense, if you have a ready supply of inexpensive fruit available.

Drying concentrates the sugars and fibres in the fruit so if you use dried fruit, your smoothy will be a little sweeter than one made with fresh fruit and you'll find that the fibre provides more, shall we say, 'cleansing power'! When you use dried fruit in a smoothie recipe, it's a good idea to rehydrate the fruit by covering it with just enough water in a saucepan and heating slowly. When the fruits have become plump, allow them to cool and drain. You can keep the liquid to use in another recipe! Chop the fruit before adding it to the blender.

One last thing: smoothies should be pleasurable, not a form of punishment! Look at the recipes and remember they are suggestions: if you don't like a particular fruit, then don't force yourself to eat or drink it! Have fun with the recipes: increase or decrease the amounts and proportions to suit your tastes.

Blending

You don't need a juice extractor for the recipes in this book. Having said that, take a look at your blender or food processor and the instruction booklet that came with it. You may be surprised to find that your machine already has a special blade or attachment for dealing with extracting juice

from some fruits and vegetables.

Make sure your blender is strong enough to deal with ice cubes and frozen fruit – the instruction manual will tell you!

Most blenders have at least three settings: off, slow and fast. Start blending smoothies on a slow speed and then move up to fast to whizz them into a frenzy.

In addition to your blender, most of the gadgets and gizmos you need are probably already in your kitchen cupboards.

Weighing scales and measuring spoons are useful for when you need to keep an eye on quantities. Because of the differences between metric and imperial weights and measures, to say nothing of American cups and sticks, the measurements given in the recipes are approximate equivalents. If you find you've got more, or less, than the quantity required in the recipe, who cares! You can alter any of the recipes to suit your taste!

Chopping board: some fruit and vegetables will have to be chopped up to fit into your blender – there's no way you'll get a whole pineapple a blender!

Some extra ingredients

To make your own yoghurt:

- 1 litre (1 $\frac{3}{4}$ pint) UHT milk (whole) (I use UHT milk as it only needs warming up to blood heat (not boiling and cooling down) so it's more energy efficient!)
- 2 tbsp live, natural yoghurt
- 2 tbsp dried milk (optional, but it makes for a thicker yoghurt)

Heat the milk gently to blood heat, add the yoghurt and dried milk and mix thoroughly with a plastic spoon (not metal). Pour into a warmed vacuum flask (or into a bowl which can be covered and wrapped in a towel, and left in a warm place like an airing cupboard). Seal the flask and leave overnight. The next day, pour out of the flask into a bowl, stir, cover and chill.

For a thicker, 'Greek Style' yoghurt, pour the yoghurt from the vacuum flask and strain off the whey – the thin liquid – from the thicker yoghurt through a piece of muslin.

When you want to make your next batch of yoghurt, simply use 2 tablespoons of your own home-made yoghurt to 'start' your next batch off.

Coconut milk

You can buy coconut milk in cartons in shops – along with coconut cream – but in general, it has been highly sweetened. The tastiest and most refreshing coconut milk is that straight from the nut – because you'll have worked up a sweat cracking it open! Alternatively, you can make a coconut milk using the shredded flesh – either fresh or dried – of the coconut:

125ml ($\frac{1}{4}$ pint) grated fresh coconut flesh or 75ml (2 $\frac{1}{2}$fl oz) of dried grated coconut

2-3 drops vanilla essence

125ml ($\frac{1}{4}$ pint) boiling water

Put the coconut into the blender and add the boiling water. Blend on a low speed for around 20 seconds. Gradually (if possible) increase the speed to high and blend for another 20-30 seconds. Allow to cool then refrigerate. It will keep for about a week in the fridge.

peach & strawberry

A thick golden drink flecked with pink, you could add a splash of chilled sparkling white wine or champagne for a summer party!

ingredients

1 peach, stoned (pitted) (or use canned in own or apple juice)

1 small orange, peeled and broken into segments

6 strawberries, hulled and cut in half – fresh, frozen or canned – or raspberries if you prefer

mineral water (optional)

method

Slice the peach into the blender, add the orange segments and the strawberries. Blend until smooth, adding a dash of mineral water if too thick.

pina colada

Famous as an alcoholic cocktail, the name means 'strained pineapple', as in parts of the Caribbean it is served in a hollowed-out pineapple. It needs a bit of forward planning, as the ice cubes are made from frozen soya milk, and need to be prepared a little in advance.

175ml (about 5fl oz) coconut milk
3 slices pineapple, chopped, fresh or canned
1 kiwi fruit, chopped
6 frozen soya milk cubes

Freeze some soya milk in ice cubes trays in advance. Put the coconut milk, pineapple, kiwi fruit and the soya milk ice cubes into the blender. Blend on a low speed for around 20 seconds. Gradually (if possible) increase the speed to high and blend for another 20-30 seconds until smooth.

strawberry split

A really fruity 'slushy'! The combination of strawberries, pineapple and apple juice make for a deliciously refreshing drink. If you prefer, you can substitute sparkling mineral water for the lemonade.

ingredients

6-8 strawberries, hulled and halved

25ml (1fl oz) pineapple juice, or 1 tbsp of crushed fruit

25ml (1fl oz) apple juice

½ lime, squeezed

chilled lemonade

crushed ice

method

Put the strawberries and pineapple (or pineapple juice) into the blender along with the apple juice and the lime juice and blend until smooth. Stop the blender and add a good scoop or two of crushed ice and blend again. Pour into a tall glass and top with chilled lemonade and serve with straws.

slushy mix

Citrus fruits and berries make terrific slushies, but melons make delicious versions, too. Because they are naturally watery, you won't have to add more water. You can use fresh fruit, squeezed or pulped in the blender. To make 200ml (7fl oz) of juice you'll need about 4 oranges, 1½ grapefruits, 4 lemons, 6 limes, 1 pineapple and 275g (10oz) of berries. If you use melons, 1 honeydew melon or ½ a watermelon will be enough, and leave out the water in the recipe.

200ml (7fl oz) or so of juice

100ml (3½fl oz) water

Mix the water and the juice in a shallow container and put it in the freezer compartment for about 1 hour. Remove from the freezer and stir the ice crystals around. Place back in the freezer for another half an hour. Remove and stir again. Then its ready to use.

summer soda

This has a lovely citrus-vanilla flavour. If you like your mix a little less sweet, just omit the sugar. You can use ready-made ice cream or you could make your own.

ingredients

25ml (1fl oz) orange juice, or ½ orange squeezed
25ml (1fl oz) grapefruit juice, ½ small grapefruit, squeezed
½ lemon, squeezed
1 tsp sugar
1 scoop vanilla ice cream
75ml (3fl oz) chilled soda or mineral water
broken ice

method

Dissolve the sugar in the juices and add with the soda or mineral water, to a tall glass a quarter filled with broken ice. Float the ice cream on the top and add some straws and a spoon.

tail feathers

Another classic 'mocktail', this time based on the Highball, a long drink first devised by New York bartender, Patrick Duffy in 1895. The chopped mint dispersed throughout the drink is really refreshing. If you prefer, you can substitute mineral water for the ginger ale.

ingredients

125ml (4fl oz) orange juice, or 3 oranges squeezed

2 limes, squeezed

2-3 leaves of fresh mint, chopped

chilled ginger ale to top

crushed ice

method

Mix the orange juice with the lime juice and chopped mint. Half fill a glass with plenty of crushed ice and pour over the fruit mix. Top with a little chilled ginger ale and decorate with a sprig of mint.

grenadine frappé

Very simple, but very refreshing. Grenadine is made from the juice of pomegranates and gives mixed drinks a gorgeous pink colour as well as a fruity sweetness. Make sure your grenadine is zero-alcohol if you don't want a boozy blend!

ingredients

I scoop lemon sherbet (see recipe on page 486)

I lime, squeezed

I tbsp grenadine

slice of lime and a sprig of mint to garnish

method

Mix the grenadine and lime juice together. Put the sherbet into a glass and pour the juice mix over the top. Decorate with the lime slice and the mint sprig.

pineapple & orange slushy

Another very simple mix. Follow the quantities given for the slushy mix on page 461, then add the pineapple juice and you will end up with two good-sized servings of delicious slushy.

ingredients

For 2 servings:

orange slushy mix (see recipe on page 461)

200ml (about 7fl oz) pineapple juice

method

Divide the slushy mix between two glasses and drizzle the pineapple juice over the top.

avalanche

This is another very simple, but wonderfully refreshing drink for hot days. You can use lemon or lime sorbet for this. For a 'boozy smoothie', you could even add a splash of gin.

ingredients

1 scoop lemon sherbet (see recipe on page 486)
chilled bitter lemon
2-3 slices of lime
crushed ice

method

Fill a tall glass half full with crushed ice, slipping two of the lime slices into the glass as well. Pop the scoop of lemon sherbet on top. Top up with a little chilled bitter lemon and decorate with the last lime slice.

frozen barbie

Yes it's pink! Use the slushy mix recipe on page 475 and this recipe will serve two 'living dolls'. Watermelon are in fact botanically unrelated to 'true' melons (which include pumpkins and cucumbers). Nevertheless there are few tastier – or more refreshing – fruits.

ingredients

For two servings:

strawberry slushy mix (see page 461)

½ watermelon, de-seeded and chopped

method

Scoop the flesh out of the watermelon and pass it through a sieve to separate the seeds, or just pick them out one by one, and purée the flesh in the blender. Add the slushy mix and stir gently, then divide between two glasses.

pear pastis

Pastis, from the French word for 'mixture', is a liquorice-flavoured liquor which, when mixed with water, becomes cloudy. While this version doesn't have the alcohol content, it does look a little like a pastis and it does make use of star anise for the flavour!

ingredients

3 tbsp water

3-4 star anise, crushed

½ tbsp caster sugar

2 pears, fresh (peeled and cored) or canned, chopped

chilled sparkling mineral water

method

Crush the star anise and place in a small saucepan. Add the sugar and 3 tablespoons of water and bring to the boil. Stirring the mix, let it bubble for about 2 minutes. Remove from the heat and allow to stand for about 10 minutes. Chop the pear flesh, place in the blender and blend until smooth. Strain the star anise liquor through a fine sieve and pour it into the pear mix. Stir well. Put the pear mix into a tall glass and top with sparkling chilled mineral water and serve immediately.

frozen melon

Melons are watery fruits and therefore really refreshing. Using the quantities given for the slushy mix (see page 179) this will serve two thirsty people. Cantaloupe melons have a lovely golden-coloured flesh and the fruit is full of carotenoids which are believed to inhibit the growth of cancer cells.

ingredients

For 2 servings:

orange slushy mix (see page 461)

½ cantaloupe melon, de-seeded and chopped

method

Put the melon into the blender and blend until smooth. Divide the orange slushy mix between two glasses and pour the melon juice over the top.

granizado de cassis

Cassis is the French for blackcurrants, from which the liqueur crème de cassis is made. You can use this, or if you prefer a non-alcoholic version, use a blackcurrant cordial instead.

ingredients

20ml (about ¼fl oz) blackcurrant cordial or crème de cassis

½ orange, squeezed

chilled soda or mineral water

crushed ice

method

Put the blackcurrant cordial into a glass and mix in the orange juice. Fill the glass a quarter full with crushed ice and top with a dash or two of chilled soda or mineral water.

You can also make a Granadizo de Limon, a lime version of this drink: use Rose's Lime Juice and the squeezed juice of half a fresh lime in place of the cassis/blackcurrant.

crème de menthe

Not the alcoholic liqueur, but a minty iced yoghurt smoothie – although you could add a dash if you wish. Mint is not only an excellent digestive aid, it also helps to relieve headaches, especially those caused by stress, so this is a terrific way to chill out!

1 small bunch of mint, about 8 leaves, chopped finely
100ml (3½fl oz) yoghurt
crushed ice

Chop the mint finely, reserving a sprig for garnish. Put the yoghurt into the blender and sprinkle in the chopped mint. Blend until smooth and the mint is well distributed. If it is a little too thick, add a dash of cold milk and blend again. Put some crushed ice into a glass and pour over the yoghurt mix. Pop a sprig of mint on top and serve straightaway.

virgin snowball

A true snowball contains advocaat, a brandy-and-egg liqueur made in Holland. This vanilla-flavoured confection is equally nice!

ingredients

1 apple, peeled, cored and chopped

2-3 drops vanilla essence

8 frozen plain yoghurt ice cubes (see page 31 for recipe)

method

Put the apple into the blender and purée it until smooth. Add the vanilla essence and 3 of the frozen yoghurt cubes. Blend, then stop and stir, then add 3 more frozen yoghurt cubes. Blend again then stop, stir and add the remaining cubes and blend again briefly. Serve immediately.

virgin raspberry daiquiri

This recipe calls for raspberry syrup which is widely available in supermarkets. Look for it next to the ice cream chests! If you don't have any to hand, you can use half a tablespoon of the syrup from a can of raspberries instead!

ingredients

60g (about 2½oz) raspberries, fresh, frozen or canned

50ml (about 2fl oz) pineapple juice, or 1 slice canned fruit

½ lemon, squeezed

1 tsp caster sugar

½ tbsp raspberry syrup

2 scoops crushed ice

method

Put the raspberries and the pineapple into the blender and blend until smooth. Add the lemon juice, the sugar and the raspberry syrup and blend again. Put 2 scoops of crushed ice in the blender and stir the mix together. Pour into a glass and garnish with a raspberry or two!

pink pineapple

Pineapples are not fruits in the ordinary sense of the word: they are, in fact, multiple organs that form when the fruits of around one hundred flowers coalesce!

ingredients

1/4 pineapple (or 3 thick slices of canned fruit in its own juice, drained)

1 orange, a blood orange will add an even deeper colour

150g (5oz) strawberries

method

Peel the pineapple and the orange. Wash the strawberries and remove the stalks. Place the fruit into a blender and blend together until smooth. Garnish with a strawberry – if there are any left!

full tank

This really is 'breakfast in a glass', and makes a good 300ml (½ pint) serving. You can use fresh pineapple, or substitute with canned fruit, but make sure it's in its own juice, not in sugary syrup. Again, if you don't have a juicer to tackle the apple, you can still whizz it in a blender/food processor, or even use a dash of ready made juice, organic of course!

ingredients

¼ pineapple, or about 100g (3½ oz) of canned pineapple in its own juice

1 small apple, or a good dash of ready-made, pressed organic apple juice

100ml (3½fl oz) soya milk

1 small handful of alfalfa sprouts

ice cube

method

Remove the skin from the pineapple, if using fresh, and wash, core and chop the apple. Place the fruit and the alfalfa sprouts in the blender/food processor and blend until smooth. Add the soya milk and ice cube and blend again briefly. Serve in a tall glass and sprinkle a few alfalfa sprouts on top to garnish.

orange pear

A very simple and delicious drink, guaranteed to help you unwind and de-stress at the end of a long day. Pears are a good source of pectin – a great bowel regulator – and they sweep cholesterol from the body.

ingredients

3 oranges

1 pear

method

Peel the oranges and remove the stalk from the pear. Cut into chunks and place the fruit in a blender/food processor. Blend on a low speed for around 20 seconds. Gradually (if possible) increase the speed to high and blend for another 20-30 seconds. Pour into a glass and garnish with a slice of orange.

wake-up call

If absolutely nothing but coffee will get you up and at it in the morning, then try this delicious, spicy iced coffee. It's especially good in summer, but is also a nice way to enjoy a midday or post-lunch coffee!

ingredients

1/2 tbsp freshly ground coffee
1/2 tsp ground nutmeg
1/2 tsp ground cardamom
250ml (1/2 pint) boiling water
1 tbsp vanilla ice cream
1/2 tbsp honey
ice cubes
sprinkle of cardamom to garnish

method

Put the coffee, nutmeg and cardamom into a heatproof bowl and pour on the boiling water. Leave to stand until cold. Strain into blender/food processor and blend with ice cream and honey. Pour into a glass over ice cubes and sprinkle with a little ground cardamom.

waterfall

Grapes, pears and melons are delicious when combined and they have the added bonus of 'strengthening' the kidneys. If you can't get your hands on grapes, use a couple of apples instead.

ingredients

125g (4oz) green or yellow grapes, cut into halves

2 pears, cored and chopped, fresh or canned

1/4 cantaloupe melon, peeled, de-seeded and chopped

pinch of ground ginger

method

Wash and dry the grapes and cut them into half. Put the grapes, the pear flesh and the chopped melon into the blender. Blend on a low speed for around 20 seconds. Gradually (if possible) increase the speed to high and blend for another 20-30 seconds. If the mixture is a little too thick for your taste, add a splash of apple or white grape juice. Dust with a pinch of ground ginger.

very berry best

This mix combines some of the tastiest fruits, fruits which we all too often think of as an indulgence. The total cost is probably no more than a cup of take-away coffee and it's so much better for your health. You can vary the quantities and types of berries as you like. Just choose your favourites!

ingredients

75g (about 2oz or so) raspberries – fresh, frozen or canned

75g (about 2oz or so) blueberries – fresh, frozen or canned

75g (about 2oz or so) pitted cherries – fresh, canned or bottled

75g (about 2oz or so) grapes, cut in half

1 pear, or a slice of melon, peeled and chopped

method

Put the berries, cherries and grapes into the blender. Add the chopped pear or melon. Blend on a low speed for around 20 seconds. Gradually (if possible) increase the speed to high and blend for another 20-30 seconds.

raspberry nectar

Rich in Vitamin B, this lovely drink will 'de-frazzle' nerves and give a well-deserved boost to both body and spirit, especially when you smell the lovely scents of fruit and lemon balm or mint.

ingredients

80g (3oz) raspberries, fresh, frozen or canned

1 peach, fresh or canned

sprig of mint

method

Rinse the raspberries and pat dry. De-stone the peach and cut into quarters. Place the fruit in a blender. Blend on a low speed for around 20 seconds. Gradually (if possible) increase the speed to high and blend for another 20-30 seconds. Pour into a glass and decorate with a sprig of mint.

smooth passion

A really pronounced passion fruit flavour – something to be savoured slowly! The sweet, golden flesh of passion fruits has many black but edible seeds that can't be separated unless you strain the fruit – but then you will lose the many minerals they contain!

ingredients

2 passion fruits

1 small banana

1 orange

200ml (7fl oz) natural, live yoghurt

method

Cut the passion fruits in half and scoop out the flesh. Peel and break the banana into chunks. Peel and break the orange into segments. Place all the fruit into the blender with the yoghurt. Blend on a low speed for around 20 seconds. Gradually (if possible) increase the speed to high and blend for another
20-30 seconds.

raspberry relief

Raspberries are astringent and protect the gut from inflammation. They, like honey, have natural antibiotics, helping to fight off infecting organisms in the gut.

ingredients

100g (4oz) raspberries

2 large tbsp natural, live yoghurt

1-2 tsp of honey

2 tbsp milk

method

Put all the ingredients into a blender/food processor and blend together. Pour into a glass. Garnish with a few berries if you like.

pineapple-almond

A delicious way to beat stress and boost your energy levels. Weight for weight, almonds have one-third more protein than eggs! They also have B Vitamins which are vital for nerve function.

ingredients

1 tbsp ground almonds

1 tbsp grated coconut

1/4 pineapple, peeled (or 3 thick slices of canned pineapple in own juice, drained)

150ml (3 1/2fl oz) natural live yoghurt

method

Purée the almonds and coconut in a blender/food processor with the pineapple. Add the yoghurt and blend again. Pour into a glass and sprinkle with a few flaked almonds.

mango & orange smoothie

A gorgeous, silky smooth combination of sweet mango and sharp orange. For more than 4,000 years in their native India, mangoes have been used to treat diabetes and high blood pressure.

ingredients

½ mango fresh or canned

1 orange, peeled and broken into segments

100ml (3½ fl oz) natural, live yoghurt

squeeze of lime juice

method

Peel and break the orange into segments and chop the mango into pieces. Place in the blender and squeeze on the lime juice. Blend until smooth and then add the yoghurt. Blend on a low speed for around 20 seconds. Gradually (if possible) increase the speed to high and blend for another 20-30 seconds.

apple smoothie

Smoothies made with live natural yoghurt and fresh fruit juices are a great way to start the day and help to maintain the balance of 'good bacteria' in your gut. Whether detoxing or weight-watching, it is vital that your body is nourished. You need to replace vital vitamins and minerals, and energise your body to keep it working efficiently.

ingredients

1 apple, cored and chopped

2 oranges (or 1 small glass of orange juice)

100ml (31/2 fl oz) natural live yoghurt

10 small mint leaves, finely chopped

method

Wash, core and chop the apple and peel the oranges. Pour the yoghurt into a blender/food processor and add the fruit. Blend until smooth. Sprinkle with chopped mint leaves and garnish with a slice of orange if you like. If you want a longer drink, add a splash or two of chilled mineral water.

sherbet

This sweet but tangy sherbet is made with equal parts sugar and water/fruit juice. I've used the word 'cup' here for the measure: if your cup holds 125ml (3½fl oz) you'll end up with 250ml (½ pint) of sherbet, enough for two good scoops!

ingredients

2 cups sugar

1 cup water

1 cup fruit juice, for example orange, lemon, lime (or lemon-lime), or pink

grapefruit, and some of the grated zest of the fruit

You can also make sherbet with pineapple or 'berry juice', such as blackcurrant, raspberry or cranberry.

method

Dissolve 2 cups of sugar in 1 cup of water and simmer gently in a small saucepan for 2-3 minutes. Add 1 cup of citrus fruit juice and the grated zest of the fruit and allow to cool. Then freeze in a suitable container. When ready, the sherbet should have a firm, ice cream texture.

Try layering two or three small scoops of each sherbet in a glass for a variety of flavours. Press the sherbets into the glass on top of each other and chill the glass again in the freezer before serving.

passion cooler

Passion fruit has a glorious flavour, although many people are put off by the seeds. You can strain the fruit through a sieve if you want a seedless version, or use passion fruit juice.

ingredients

50ml (2fl oz) pineapple juice, or 2 sliced fruit, chopped

50ml (2fl oz) mango juice, or half a mango, chopped

25ml (1fl oz) or 1/2 orange, squeezed

25ml (1fl oz) passion fruit juice or 1 passion fruit

1/2 banana, peeled and chopped

crushed ice

method

Put the banana, the orange juice, the mango and pineapple juice (or fruit) into the blender with the passion fruit (or juice) and blend until smooth. Stop the blender and add a good scoop of crushed ice and blend again. Pour into a glass and serve immediately.

bora-bora

This inspired drink takes its name from Bora Bora, the tiny South Pacific island in the Society Islands, northwest of Tahiti. Good things often come in small packages!

ingredients

74ml (3fl oz) pineapple juice, or 2-3 slices of fruit, canned
    or fresh

1 tbsp grenadine

½ lime, squeezed

chilled dry ginger ale to top

crushed ice

method

Put the pineapple juice (or fruit) into the blender with the lime juice and grenadine. Blend until smooth. Stop the blender and add a good scoop of crushed ice and blend briefly until mixed. Pour into a glass and top with a little chilled, dry ginger ale and serve with straws.

kiwi-lime fizz

Limes have the most gorgeous scent and flavour and they make perfect partners for sweet ripe kiwi fruits, also known as 'Chinese gooseberries'. Kiwis have twice as much Vitamin C as an orange and more fibre than an apple, and they are rich in potassium. Lack of this mineral can lead to high blood pressure, chronic fatigue and depression.

1 scoop of lime sherbet (see page 486 for recipe)

1 kiwi fruit, peeled and chopped

1 fresh lime, squeezed

Put the lime sherbet in the blender with the chopped kiwi and the lime juice and blend briefly on a low speed.

fruity fantasy

This is just gorgeous: it's a terrific 'party punch' that's easy to make in volume.

ingredients

75ml (3fl oz) orange juice or one large orange, peeled and broken into segments

50ml (2fl oz) pineapple juice or one thick slice of fruit, chopped

1 kiwi fruit, peeled and chopped

4 strawberries, hulled and halved

2 tbsp melon

2 scoops crushed ice

method

Put the orange and pineapple (or juices) into the blender with the kiwi and strawberries. Add two scoops of melon and blend until smooth. Stop the blender and add 2 good scoops of crushed ice and blend briefly. Pour into a glass and serve with straws. Garnish with some of the fruit, too, if you have some to spare!

Index

bibliography

Peter Bohrmann **The Bartender's Guide** *Greenwich Editions, 2004*

David Briggs **The Cocktail Handbook** *New Holland, 1999*

Salvatore Calabrese **Classic Cocktails** *Prion, 1997*

Maria Costantino **The Cocktail Handbook** D & S Books

Maria Costantino **Cocktails Deluxe** D & S Books

Robert Cross **The Classic 1,000 Cocktail Recipes** *Foulsham, 2003*

Davis A Embury **The Fine Art of Mixing Drinks** *Faber, 1963*

Ambrose Heath **Good Drinks** *Faber, 1939*

Michael Jackson **Michael Jackson's Pocket Bar Book** *Mitchell Bea* 1981

Michael Jackson **Michael Jackson's Bar & Cocktail Book** *Mitchel Beazley, 2002*

Brian Lucas **365 Cocktails** *Duncan Baird, 2003*

Harry MacElhone with Andrew MacElhone **Harry's ABC of Mixing Cocktails** *Souvenir Press, 1986*

Gary Regan **The Bartender's Bible** *Harper Collins, 1993*

Ian Wisniewski **Party Cocktails** *Conran Octopus, 2002*

credits & acknowledgements

Thanks to Paul for the pictures, Ena for her fridge, Brain for the plumbing, Jo Locke for 'taste-testing' and Isabel in the wines and spirits department of Selfridges, Oxford Street, London, for her knowledge, enthusiasm and delivery service!

Finally, a big thank-you to all those who generously provided insight and recipes on their web sites.

www.kingcocktail.com

(Dale DeGroff, acknowledged as the one of the world's – if not the world's – greatest living bartenders.)

www.cocktails.about.com

(Newsletter, history, recipes, trivia and party games!)

www.cocktaildb.com

(Martin Doudroff's and Ted (Dr. Cocktail) Haigh's extensive database of recipes, and a great message board, too!)

Remember, please drink responsibly